Other books by the same authors:

EDMUND KEELEY   *The Libation*
                             The Gold-Hatted Lover

PHILIP SHERRARD   *Orientation and Descent*
                             The Marble Threshing Floor:
                               Studies in Modern Greek Poetry
                             Athos, the Mountain of Silence
                             The Greek East and the Latin West:
                               a Study in the Christian Tradition

Six Poets of Modern Greece

SIX POETS OF
MODERN GREECE

Chosen, translated, and introduced by

EDMUND KEELEY

AND PHILIP SHERRARD

ALFRED A. KNOPF · NEW YORK

1961

UNESCO COLLECTION OF CONTEMPORARY WORKS

European Series

THIS IS A BORZOI BOOK,
PUBLISHED BY ALFRED A. KNOPF, INC.

FIRST AMERICAN EDITION

This book has been accepted in the Translations Series of Contemporary Works jointly sponsored by the International PEN Club and the United Nations Educational, Scientific and Cultural Organization (UNESCO).

L. C. catalog card number: 61–11505

for M. *and* A.

PREFACE

DURING recent years there has been a steadily growing awareness that the Greek world is still producing poetry of a distinction and urgency that command attention—an awareness revealed in the increasing number of isolated translations of individual poets and in the publication of critical studies and appreciations. But until now there has been no adequate attempt to present to the English-speaking world any really representative selection from this poetry. It is this which our volume seeks to offer. The six poets whose work is here included are by no means the only Greek poets of significance who have written during this century; but they are certainly those through whom the Greek experience in the modern world is expressed most powerfully. Their work, it seems to us, does full justice to the complexity, richness, and depth of that experience. The actual choice of individual poems has naturally been dictated to an extent by the exigencies of translation: certain poems, as good in the original as anything offered here, have had to be omitted simply because in translation they have seemed to suffer more than others; yet we have tried to include only poems which are both important in themselves and representative of the individual poet's best work. We have also tried to avoid any distortion of the poems through attempts to reproduce their rhyme or metre: only when this could be done with no forcing have we permitted it. Our aim throughout has been a translation which communicates above all the sense of the original in the most direct and appropriate language. In this way we have hoped to express the experience of the poetry in a form which is both faithful to the poet and vivid to the English reader.

We wish to express our gratitude, for their co-operation and assistance, to Mrs. Anna Sikelianos, Mr. George Seferis, Mr. D. I. Antoniou, Mr. Odysseus Elytis, Mr. Nikos Gatsos, Mr. Alexander

Singopoulos, and Mr. George Savides; to the Hogarth Press, publishers of *The Poems of C. P. Cavafy*, translated by John Mavrogordato; and to the Rockefeller Foundation, the Princeton University Research Committee, St. Antony's College, Oxford, and the Guggenheim Foundation. Versions of translations included in this volume have appeared in *New Directions 14, Colonnade, Encounter, Nine, Partisan Review, Accent, Comparative Literature, The Beloit Poetry Journal, Perspective, The Antioch Review, The Western Review, Chicago Review, Prairie Schooner, The Colorado Quarterly, The Western Humanities Review, The Charioteer,* and *The Transatlantic Review.*

E. K.
P. S.

Katounia, Limni

CONTENTS

CONTENTS

CONTENTS

Six Poets of Modern Greece

INTRODUCTION

WHEN the Greek War of Independence broke out in 1821, two poets, Dionysios Solomos and Andreas Kalvos, had already begun to give expression to the re-awakening consciousness of the Greek people. Throughout the nineteenth century other poets followed these pioneers, all working in a tradition whose roots, set in the age-old demotic Greek heritage, were native and local in the best sense. The prolific master Kostis Palamas, writing his major work round the end of the century, was perhaps the most influential of these. In a way, his work marks a turning point. The strongly romantic and optimistic temper of the nineteenth century, which Palamas fully expresses, now gives place to new attitudes. On the one hand, Anghelos Sikelianos, while remaining essentially faithful to the local Greek tradition, seeks to give it new depth by incorporating into his poetry the intellectual vision of ancient religious traditions. On the other hand, the Alexandrian poet Constantine Cavafy introduces an element of matter-of-fact irony which, gently but effectively, confronts the reader with a human situation that, whatever else it may be, is neither romantic nor optimistic.

From the point of view of the native Greek tradition in which Solomos, Kalvos, and Palamas all wrote, the poetry of Constantine Cavafy (1863–1933), a selection from which opens this anthology, might scarcely seem to be Greek at all. Its background is very different from that of these other poets. Indeed, to begin with, it scarcely appears to have any real background of its own, and the early poems in the main do little more than reflect the fashionable literary attitudes of the last decades of the nineteenth century. Behind them one can discern the compound but somewhat etiolated shadow of such figures as Gautier, Henri Murger, Huysmans, Wilde and Pater: aesthetic, feminine, haunted by a sense of corruption, indifferent to if not scornful

3

of nature, fastidious, devoted to art as the expression and stimulant of fine sensations, and looking upon works of art as little more than a superior and sophisticated form of aphrodisiac:

I do not want real narcissi—nor lilies
do I like, nor real roses:
the banal, the common gardens they adorn,
their flesh gives me bitterness, fatigue, and pain—
I am bored with their perishable charms.
Give me artificial flowers—the glories of metal and glass—
which neither wither nor rot, with shapes that do not age.
Flowers from the splendid gardens of another country
where Theories, and Rhythms, and Knowledge live.

Flowers I love kneaded of glass and gold
of faithful Art the faithful gifts;
with colours more beautifully tinted than those of nature,
and wrought with mother-of-pearl and enamel,
with leaves and stems ideal.
They draw their grace from wise and purest Aestheticism;
they do not sprout in the filth of earth and mud.

If they have no aroma we shall douse them with fragrance,
we shall burn before them oils of perfume.

Some of the early poems have a certain elegance and polish, but they all share, as we have noted, one central weakness: Cavafy wrote them without possessing any real personal background, without having made his own a "landscape" of figures, of visibilia, with wider terms of reference than those provided by the rootless *fin de siècle* aestheticism whose moods and attitudes he sought to express. It is always one of the major tasks of a poet to provide himself with such a "landscape," and when

4

society possesses a tradition, the images and symbols of which are common to the great majority of the people, this task is relatively simple; when there is no such tradition, it is considerably more difficult. Collective myths, collective terms of reference, lose their hold, the poet no longer shares any recognized background of imagery with the rest of society, and, whether he likes it or not, he is forced more and more into isolation. If at the same time, as is often the case, he is unable to discover for himself any purpose that transcends his individuality, and has therefore nothing left to value but what concerns the life of the senses only, his poetry is in danger of becoming the mere indulgence of private sentiment and emotion.

It was in a situation such as this that Cavafy found himself. Condemned—whether by choice or by fate is not the question— to that kind of aesthetic life which had been the interest of those figures under whose influence he wrote his first poems, how, in giving expression to this life, could he yet avoid falling back on the already debased language and imagery of an effete romanticism? Where could he find the landscape of figures, the visibilia, adequate to his purpose? As we have suggested, Cavafy had no relationship with the Greek demotic tradition on which poets like Solomos and Sikelianos, for instance, could draw with such fruitfulness; to pretend that he had would merely have meant substituting one alien background for another. In any case, the Greek demotic tradition was fundamentally heroic and patriotic, and as such was hardly likely to appeal to Cavafy, who, a colonial Greek, was little concerned with the political destiny of a new Greece; his pessimistic vision foresaw a future of conquest, decay, and death from which relief could be found only in present aesthetic pleasure, in a stoic reserve, and in the recollection of a past already long since perished.

Just how Cavafy lighted on the "landscape" through which he could speak with greater point and freedom, it is difficult to say. But it may have been that in the modern Alexandria in which he lived there were enough visible reminders of and asso-

5

ciations with an older Alexandria to stimulate his curiosity and to suggest that *recherche du temps perdu* which his poetry was increasingly to become. It may have been that in the mixed races and the confusion of tongues, in the Christian churches and the pagan ruins, in the bustle of the port and in the bargaining of merchants in bazaar and market of his contemporary environment, there was enough to lead Cavafy to discover, largely through reading, a whole vanished world in which he could see, as in a mirror, the faithful reflection of that human condition which it was his desire to portray. At all events, behind the mercantilism of present-day Alexandria, Cavafy began to discern the lineaments of the great hellenistic Alexandria, the capital of the Ptolemies, centre of a flourishing kingdom and a rich terrain, peopled by Greek, Jew, Egyptians, by all the races of the Middle East. The Alexandria which Cavafy "discovered" was in fact the crown and focus of that extraordinary hellenistic world which included also such famed cities as Antioch and Jerusalem, Seleukeia and Ephesus, and numbered kingdoms like those of Syria, of Media, of Commagene, and of Macedonia itself, from which, with the conquests of Alexander the Great, all had begun. It was a curious, chequered world, knit mainly by the common Greek language. "Then he was that best of things," Cavafy was to write, " a Hellene: mankind has no quality more precious." And in a mock-serious poem he celebrates the expedition which gave the word Hellene the status it had in the world of which Alexandria was the centre:

> And from that amazing all-Greek expedition,
> the victorious, the brilliant,
> the much talked of, the glorified
> as no other has ever been glorified,
> the incomparable, we ourselves emerged:
> the great new hellenic world.

INTRODUCTION

> We: the Alexandrians, the Antiochians,
> the Seleukeians, and the countless
> other Greeks of Egypt and of Syria,
> and those of Media, and of Persia, and all the rest.
> With the far-reaching domination,
> with the many-sided activity of prudent assimilation,
> and the Common Greek Tongue
> which we carried into Bactria, to the Indians.

It was in this hellenistic Alexandrian world, then, that Cavafy found the "landscape" through which he could express himself with pertinence and urbanity. Out of it he was to build his "myth" of a personal and at the same time perennial human condition, that of the tired, rapacious, over-refined man who is the generic hero of his poems, *homo Europaeus,* as we might call him, of our not so late humanist period. For that after all is the principal figure that emerges from behind the many masks which Cavafy gives him: the sick guest of an aesthetic city, of a Greco-Roman asylum, full of selfish desires and absurd vanities, ageing into impotence and ugliness, purified by every longing, sapped by every depravity, all sentiment and all fatigue, devoted to fate and pain as the morphinist to his drug, lonely, hollowed out, old as the ages, all nostalgia, animal and sage, all bare, with no ambitions, gnawed by the dread of death, by the relentless dance of time that sweeps all that he loves into oblivion, and finding relief only in his art where he can watch with something approaching a detached irony the spectacle of a life of pleasure, folly, misfortune, vice, and sybaritic elegance which he now can never again enjoy. The poems included here, all in Cavafy's mature voice, express different aspects of his aesthetic city and the life of which it was the centre.

* * *

We have suggested that Cavafy, in creating his own landscape and his own tradition, remained isolated from both the contemporary Greek scene and the main currents of the Greek tradition; in contrast, Anghelos Sikelianos (1884–1951), turned to exactly those sources that Cavafy had ignored.

There are two main aspects to the poetry of Sikelianos. On the one hand, there is the lyric assertion of the natural world and of the human body as part of it. On the other hand, there is the austere vision of the seer who knows that the natural world is full of tragedy and suffering and that the true centre of man's life is elsewhere. There is a refusal to deny the senses, a suspicion of all renunciation and asceticism; and there is the lifting up, as it were, into an intensity of contemplation in which all earth-life is forgotten. There is the celebration of, and the insistence on, the holiness of life's spontaneous manifestations and energies; and there is the formal and hieratic awareness of a divine order, a conviction that man's failure to realise and to conform his life to this order leads to ultimate calamity. Both aspects belong to the total experience of the poetry, and the poems that follow have been selected with this in mind.

The first group in this selection are from among Sikelianos's earlier poems, and for the most part are representative of the first aspect of his poetry: the lyrical assertion of the natural world and its beauty. They are simple, direct, unaffected. Things are seen with a clear eye, with clear senses, with feelings undulled by custom and fixed routine. There is an immediate and reciprocal relationship between the poet and the world he describes, the lands and seas of Greece. Nature and natural events are felt as part of the poet's own subjective experience; the poet's life and the life of nature mingle:

> The lightning I encountered
> before it left the cloud. At the sound
> of the thunder-bolt echoed
> the first heart-beat of my joy;

at light awakenings,
at the sudden rustle of leaves,
at the full peal of bells,
at the night quietness of crickets,
at the first talk in the road
at morning, at the first windows
of the fishermen opening, at the rising
deep from the trees of many birds,
at dawn scents,
and at the sudden
ring of the breeze which sounds
in space, at the spring's gush
which fills
the golden pitcher of my love!

These early poems represent a phase in the poet's growth to maturity. This growth is not that of the mind alone; it is much more organic than that. It is the growth of the whole person, body and soul together, instinct and mind together, an awakening and overflowing of an integral sense of life. At the same time there is implicit even in this early poetry what one might call a "mythological" attitude towards life, a sense that there are certain more than natural forces at work in the universe, giving meaning and reality to the world perceived through the senses. There is a supernatural world as well as a natural world, there is the invisible as well as the visible. Not that these two worlds are opposed to, or radically separated from, one another. Rather, the natural world is penetrated by the forces of the supernatural world; it is in some sense an expression of these forces. Man's life is seen as incomplete and thwarted if he fails to realize this, if he persists in living as if the natural world, that which he can observe through his senses and with his mind, is the only world. His real fulfilment and purpose can only be achieved through a growing awareness of supernatural realities, through the growth of spiritual insight. Here the other aspect of Sikelianos's poetry comes into its own, that which expresses the poet's search for and perception of a divine order. But the impulse for this search, for this act of creative understanding, comes from experience of the natural world. From direct, sensual contact with living things man draws in the vital nourishment for his own life. This is the sap that feeds his growth, that stimulates new organs of perception. Intense physical delight turns into an illumination of the mind.

Sikelianos derived what we have called the "mythological" attitude towards life, implicit even in his early poetry, from the people of Greece and their immediate tradition. The lives of the people—harsh, poor, cruel as they often were—still possessed, in the time of Sikelianos's youth, a poetry, a vitality, a feeling of reverence and wonder before creation which had been largely lost in the West (and which have since been largely lost in Greece). Above all, the people of Sikelianos's youth had preserved through the centuries a wealth of song, legend, and dance in which were enshrined the perceptions and understandings, the qualities of thought and feeling, of a way of life whose roots went far back into the past.

Participation in a tradition such as that of the Greek people is of the utmost value for the poet. Even if he is unaware of the true nature of the wisdom it preserves, his attitude towards, and his sense of, life will nevertheless be permeated by it; his poetry, although unconsciously, will reflect it. This would seem to be what happened in Sikelianos's case. He had the good fortune to be born into a Greece where the traditional memory was still alive, where the traditional pattern of life still flourished, and where he found an ancient soul and an ancient aura. Instinctively he turned towards it. He mixed his life with its life, his roots with the roots which nourished the lives of the people:

> And to the people I descended;
> and the doors of the houses
> opened so quietly

as if the doors of a tomb.
And it was as if they embraced me
returning from the grave—
thus
the fates the thread had woven—
or as if for me the dead
had come alive again:
so deep in the ground did our roots mingle,
so were our branches raised
into the heavens.

Some of Sikelianos's most beautiful poems are those in which he draws upon and expresses aspects of the lives and customs of the Greek people as he knew them: the extract from the long poem, "The Village Wedding," in the following selection bears witness to this.

But it is one thing to write poetry which expresses—as Sikelianos's early poetry does express—a mythological attitude towards life, and another to have full and conscious understanding of the principles upon which such an attitude depends. Or, to put this another way: Sikelianos had found in the Greece into which he was born a living tradition of ideas, images, and symbols which had been preserved, even though in a confused fashion, in the memory of the people, in their legend, poetry, and dance. He had been nourished by this tradition and this memory; they had become part of him, and his responses and attitudes had to a large extent been determined by them. Since the process had in a way been an unconscious one, his task now was to make it conscious, to discover the true nature of those ideas, images, and symbols still implicit in the people's tradition. For this tradition itself was preserving in an incomplete and fragmentary way a knowledge which on a higher level had been lost. What was this knowledge and where could it be found in its more complete form? "The problem was then for me," Sikelianos writes of this stage in his development. "By what way and with what means could I achieve essential contact with and understanding of this tradition?"

His search for this contact and understanding led him to pre-Socratic Greece. It seemed to him that in this period the true nature of that mythological attitude towards life implicit in his early poems—as in the art, beliefs and customs of the Greek people—had been consciously formulated and enshrined. Orphism, the teaching of Pythagoras, the Mysteries of Eleusis, all bore witness to this, as did the poetry of Pindar and Aeschylus. In all these, Sikelianos saw expressed what was essentially the same understanding of life, an understanding which transcended blood-groups and clans, upheld the brotherhood of man, and preserved a sense of unity embracing not only mankind but all living things. It was an understanding which Sikelianos determined to restore through his poetry to the modern world. For now it was no longer only a question of the poet giving expression to his own lyrical experience of life. It was also a question of bringing back to contemporary man some consciousness of those supernatural realities without which, according to the poet, his life would be thwarted and incomplete. All Sikelianos's later poetry springs from his awareness of these realities and his desire to awaken once more in others something of the insight and the fulfilment they brought him. Using for the most part images and symbols of the Orphic and Pythagorean tradition, though in later life more and more completing these with the images and symbols of Christianity, Sikelianos developed a poetry that is both visionary and tragic, rhapsodic and sombre, joyous and full of sorrow. But its last word is not one of despair; for beyond the desolation of time and place, of death itself, is always the reality of peace and reconciliation, the "mystical first glory" of life, whose presence, the poet believed, man could ignore only at the price of his own defeat. The second group of poems in the following selection are representative of the poetry Sikelianos wrote under the influence of this vision.

The "mythological" attitude of Sikelianos was essentially a

12

matter of intellectual and spiritual conviction; that of George
Seferis (b. 1900) is more a matter of sensibility, of intense, po-
etic response to the history of his race. In Seferis's poetry myth
is used not so much to transmit spiritual insight as to dramatize
a universal mood and state of mind; nor is myth used as a self-
conscious method by which shape and order are given to the
confusion and anarchy of the modern world, as it is by certain
other contemporary poets. In contrast to these latter, we find in
Seferis a poet who turns to myth more from a sense of personal
identity with his mythology than a sense of its convenience as a
means, as a method of ordering the disorder of an alien vision.

This personal sense of myth pervades the selection from
his work offered here. Throughout the selection one may discern
a central figure, a central *persona,* who "relates" the poetry. The
persona might best be seen as a sea-captain, the ghost of Odysseus, "father" of the poet. He is the voice in the two long poems,
Mythical Story and *"Thrush,"* and he serves as the poet's mask
in many of the shorter lyrics. Seferis first describes him in "On a
Foreign Verse" (1931); the sense of kinship between Odysseus
and the poet, between the mythical hero and the mariners of
Seferis's childhood in Smyrna, is apparent in the following ex-
cerpt:

It is the great Odysseus; he who had them build the wooden
      horse and so the Achaeans conquered Troy.
I imagine he is coming to explain how I too may build a wooden
      horse to conquer my Troy.

Because he speaks humbly and peacefully, without effort, one
      might say he knows me like a father
or like certain aged mariners, who, leaning against their nets, at
      a time when the wind began to rage with the fury of
      winter,

recited to me, in my childhood, the song of Erotocritos with
      tears in their eyes . . .

The captain tells the poet about "the torment you feel when the sails of your ship are inflated by memory"; about "the bitterness of seeing your companions submerged by the elements, scattered; one by one"; about "how strangely your courage returns in talking to the dead, when the living who are left to you no longer suffice." These three themes, suggested by the Odyssey myth, are among the most insistent in Seferis's poetry. They are sentiments that no doubt became particularly familiar to this poet after the loss of his childhood home in the Asia Minor disaster of 1922 and during his years away from Greece both in the diplomatic service and as an official of the exiled war-time Government; but the important thing is that they are sentiments shared by the wandering exile of all ages, and it is through the mythical background that this universal, historical extension is dramatized.

The longing of Odysseus for the return voyage to Ithaca and his memories of a distant home haunt the "I" of *Mythical Story* and *"Thrush."* Friends and relatives lost or changed, weak companions submerged or dying, are ever on the mind of Seferis's persona. As late as "Stratis the Mariner on the Dead Sea," written eleven years after the poem quoted above, we find:

> In the Dead Sea
> enemies and friends
> wife and children
> other relations
> go and find them.

Again, in "Stratis the Mariner among the Agapanthi" (1942), our modern Odysseus bemoans the fate of his "poor, idiotic" companion Elpenor, who broke his neck in a drunken fall from the roof on Circe's palace. The persona here echoes the sea captain of "On a Foreign Verse" when he cries:

14

INTRODUCTION

It is painful and difficult, the living are not enough for me
first because they do not speak, and then
because I have to ask the dead
in order to advance.

But the dead know "the language of flowers only," the flowers of
Homer's asphodel plain, where Odysseus had gone in order to
seek guidance from the shades concerning his return home to
Ithaca. Seferis's hero, trying to reach his home, finds himself
exiled in Transvaal where there are no asphodels—only agapanthi (African lilies) whose "language" he does not understand.
The agapanthi hold the dead speechless so that they cannot offer
him the guidance that will make his homeward journey possible.

A similar nostalgia and sense of alienation, illuminated by
different symbols and dramatized in a somewhat different context, inform what many critics consider to be Seferis's finest
poem, "The King of Asine." Here the mythological source is the
Iliad: a single phrase identifying the King of Asine as one of the
heroes who sailed with the expedition to Troy. The setting of
the poem is his ruined acropolis, on a bluff near Nauplia. The
phrase, now forgotten, and the king's citadel, now no more than
a graveyard of stones, come to represent all that remains of the
lost paradise which the nostalgia of the modern Odysseus con-
stantly evokes and which he perennially seeks. Behind these
symbols there is only the void of the past, the void of experience
which has now become simply memory, of emotion which time
has turned to stone—the void, finally, of the poet himself:

And the poet lingers, looking at the stones, and asks himself
does there really exist
among these ruined lines, edges, points, hollows, and curves
does there really exist
here where one meets the path of rain, wind, and ruin
does there exist the movement of the face, shape of the tender-
    ness

of those who diminished so strangely in our lives,
those who remained the shadow of waves and thoughts bound-
      less as the sea
or perhaps, no, nothing is left but the weight
the nostalgia of the weight of a living being
there where we now remain unsubstantial, bending
like the branches of an awful willow-tree heaped in the perma-
      nence of despair
while the yellow current slowly carries down rushes uprooted in
      the mud
image of a form turned to marble by the decision of an eternal
      bitterness:
the poet a void.

This poem illustrates what is perhaps the most exciting at-
tribute of Seferis's genius: his ability to capture the mood of a
current historical moment through images that evoke the history of his race, his ability to express a contemporary state of
mind in terms of the enduring qualities that define his nation:
its landscape, its literature, its tangible and legendary past. The
image of the past haunts the persona even when he becomes
most intimate and lyrical, even when the setting and occasion
that arouse him are most immediate:

And the bird that flew away last winter
with a broken wing
the shelter of life,
and the young woman who left to play
with the dogteeth of summer
and the soul which screeching sought the lower world
and the country like a large plane-leaf swept along by the tor-
      rent of the sun
with the ancient monuments and the contemporary sorrow.

A constant source, really a symbol, of the persona's nostalgia is the figure of a woman, as the passage above suggests. This

figure first appears in "Song of Love" (1930) as an apparition out of the past that comes to haunt the poem's hero with memories of an intensely sensual experience, a union, achieved at the height of fate's rising cycle and then suddenly destroyed with the downward cycle, "the cycle which brings the sorrows." The intensity of the experience is lost in "the rocking of a foreign embrace," but the memory of it persists as a heavy, recurrent rhythm—at the end of this poem and throughout the travels of the modern Odysseus. In "Stratis the Mariner Describes a Man," the man described reports: "you know, I love a woman who left for the underworld," and a bit later, "I loved a girl . . . I think they called her Vaso, Froso, or Bilio; so I forgot the sea." The apparition appears again in "15" of *Mythical Story*; it has become even less tangible than it was in "Song of Love": the fractured form of silence which the poet cannot touch and which returns, as quickly as it came, to the shadows of another world:

Beneath the plane-tree, near the water, amidst the laurel
sleep removed you and scattered you
around me, near me, without my being able to touch the whole
      of you
one as you were with your silence;
seeing your shadow grow and diminish
lose itself in the other shadows, in the other world
which released you yet held you back.

One of Seferis's latest poems, "Engomi" (1955), concludes with an apotheosis of the woman figure. She rises out of the level plain at Engomi in Cyprus "with the unripe breasts of the Virgin, a dance motionless," to vanish in the womb of the sky like an Assumption; the poet's memory is stirred by a vision of "breasts among leaves, lips moist." This fusion of the sensual and the spiritual, of the tangible and the intangible, characterizes the figure whenever she appears. To the modern Odysseus she is an image of love's highest ecstasy, an image of "the other world," the lost paradise, where love cuts time in two and where the heart has not been turned to marble by insensitivity or frustration, a world which our hero longs for and seeks during his exile but which he reaches only in memory.

This brief account of Seferis's persona might seem to substantiate the poet's own view of himself expressed in an essay on *"Thrush"*: "I am a monotonous and obstinate man who for twenty years . . . have not ceased to say the same things again and again." A more just and accurate view is that Seferis's poems, at least those offered in this selection, constitute one long work, a modern *Odyssey*, of a different and, it would seem to us, more significant nature than that of another modern Greek writer, Nikos Kazanzakis, examples of whose work we have not included in this anthology. In Seferis's Odyssey, unity and coherence are achieved by the repetition of related motifs and the presence, always, of the same central intelligence or sensibility. This central intelligence or sensibility is sometimes called Stratis the Mariner, but normally remains an anonymous "I." As heir to the ancient wandering hero, he serves as an eloquent voice for all men of our age who are tormented by a sense of alienation and who long to return to a lost paradise, that is, for all men who share the perennial experience of Odysseus.

The three poets who conclude this anthology—Antoniou, Elytis, and Gatsos—belong to the generation that flowered between the mid-thirties and the mid-forties, a rich period in Greek letters, one which has not been equalled since. It was during this period that Seferis arrived at maturity with the publication of *Mythical Story, Gymnopaidia,* his excellent translation of Eliot, his *Book of Exercises,* and his two volumes called *Log Book I* and *Log Book II;* it was also the last occasion for any sort of unity or group vitality in the Greek literary world.

There was, surprisingly, considerable activity during the occupation, but the civil war and long period of recovery which followed proved to be disruptive. Good poets went on writing as individual poets will during periods of crisis—one is reminded of Cavafy's Phernazis in the poem "Darius"—but there was nothing to give the world of letters shape, no cause or movement or organ that might serve to define the established and recognize the young: if Phernazis was still alive and singing, his critics were either dead or deaf. In the late thirties, criticism was abundant, and there were several lively reviews. The most influential of these was *Ta Nea Grammata,* under George Katsimbalis and Andreas Karantonis; here Sikelianos published some of his finest work, here Seferis's new voice found its most responsive audience—the voice that was to dominate Greek letters for the following twenty-five years—and here some of the best new poets, including Antoniou and Elytis, received their earliest encouragement.

There is something of Seferis's nostalgia in the work of D. I. Antoniou (b. 1906). Antoniou has spent most of his life at sea as an officer in the merchant marine; the context of his poetry is that of the seaman's experience: voyages to exotic harbours, the memory of distant places, the loneliness of exile, the joy and agony of the return:

> We brought you no more than stories
> of distant places, memories
> of precious things, of perfumes.
>
> Do not seek their weight upon your hands;
> your hands should be less human
> for all we held in exile;
> the experience of touch, the struggle of weight,
> exotic colours
> you should feel in our words only
> this night of our return.

Another poem begins: "Should we turn back?/—sorrow waits
for us in the past:/what you failed to exhaust on journeys,/baring your heart"; and a third: "Tonight you remembered the beginning/the evening of rain when you decided/to make experience of the nostalgia for distant places/that left us useless/
for life."

The context is familiar: the long journey and the torment
of exile are motifs which Seferis exploited thoroughly and eloquently. But the nostalgia here is more subjective: the poet's
voice is not masked by that of a persona, nor is the nostalgia
transformed, through the agency of myth, into an historical emotion, into a sense of the eternally tragic in life, as it is in Seferis.
What Antoniou gives us is a lyrical statement of a mood—a
mood that grows out of immediate experience—repeated, qualified, elaborated until it becomes a metaphor, finally a representative state of mind. He conveys in his own terms (terms that remain more personal and ultimately less profound than those of
Seferis) the feeling of loss in the wanderer who longs for the distant homeland—his "landscape beneath the southern sky"—and
the commitment to remembrance that his wandering compels.
It is, in one sense, a national state of mind, as the literature of
the period amply indicates: the experience of exile is among the
more typical for the contemporary Greek. This is what gives Antoniou's personal metaphor a broader dimension, a larger significance; his mood becomes to an extent generic, his statement of
it a contemporary definition.

Odysseus Elytis (b. 1911) appeared (in *Ta Nea Grammata*) for the first time in 1935. His earliest poetry demonstrated an enthusiasm for the manner of the French Surrealists
as profound as the enthusiasm for the technique of the French
post-Symbolists which Seferis had revealed in his first poems at
the beginning of the decade. What Elytis offered in *Ta Nea
Grammata* and his volume *Orientations* (1940) was a surrealism which had a highly personal tone and a specific local habitation; the tone was lyrical, humorous, fanciful—everything that

is young; the habitation was the landscape and climate of Greece, particularly the landscape of the Aegean islands. The quality of his lyricism and the surrealist influence are seen characteristically in "The Mad Pomegranate Tree," a lovely poem, full of song and laughter and sunlight, a celebration of the lyric spirit itself:

In these all-white courtyards where the south wind blows
Whistling through vaulted arcades, tell me, is it the mad pome-
      granate tree
That leaps in the light, scattering its fruitful laughter
With windy wilfulness and whispering, tell me, is it the mad
      pomegranate tree
That quivers with foliage newly born at dawn
Raising high its colours in a shiver of triumph?

. . . . .

In petticoats of April first and cicadas of the feast of mid-August
Tell me, that which plays, that which rages, that which can en-
      tice
Shaking out of threats their evil black darkness
Spilling in the sun's embrace intoxicating birds
Tell me, that which opens its wings on the breast of things
On the breast of our deepest dreams, is that the mad pome-
      granate tree?

The central image here—the pomegranate tree as a playful sprite who occasions all that is hopeful and gay, that is, as the embodiment of a mood—typifies what the poet himself has called the "personal mythology" of his verse: "Repeated metamorphoses—a girl that becomes fruit, a morning disposition that becomes a tree, an idea that becomes incarnate in a human form—create a personal mythology which, without divorcing itself from feeling, finds its correlation in the world of the poet's metaphysical experience." The mystery of change, the transformation of the inanimate into the human and the human into something stranger, is hardly a new theme in poetry; what surrealism did for Elytis was to give him a means of exploiting this ancient theme in terms of his contemporary landscape and his personal sensibility, a sensibility thoroughly responsive to the beauty of Greece.

The evocation of landscape and climate through surrealist images is everywhere apparent in Elytis's early verse. In this poem we have "the saffron ruffle of day/Richly embroidered with scattered songs" and the tree "Fluttering a handkerchief of leaves of cool flame,/A sea near birth with a thousand ships and more," or "adorn[ing] itself in jealousy with seven kinds of feathers,/Girding the eternal sun with a thousand blinding prisms." The sea and the sun are so consistently celebrated as to suggest a kind of pagan mysticism, a pantheism, a worship of the gods of water and light. The poet himself has said that his vision is "essentially that of the marine world of the Aegean, with a certain mystical extension that has its centre in the midday and the light." In his poems, this vision is never, of course, reduced to a theology or even a statement of faith; it is always represented by specific images or observed settings, most palpably in the volume with the significant title of *The First Sun* (1943), from which the large part of our selection comes.

The poems in this volume offer a landscape which is both typical and personal; it is the landscape of Greece highlighted by the poet's almost religious adoration:

> Drinking the sun of Corinth
> Reading the marble ruins
> Striding across vineyards and seas
> Sighting along the harpoon
> A votive fish that slips away
> I found the leaves that the psalm of the sun memorizes
> The living land that desire opens joyously.

> I drink water, cut fruit,
> Thrust my hand into the wind's foliage
> The lemon trees irrigate the pollen of summer
> The green birds tear my dreams
> I leave with a glance
> A wide glance in which the world is recreated
> Beautiful from the beginning to the dimensions of the heart!

The familiar ruins, the vineyards, the lemon trees, the sea and the sun, are all here, and so is the voice of the poet offering up a hymn in worship of what he sees. The climate too is immediately recognizable, yet even when the poet describes it in his simplest style, his description seems an act of praise:

> A long time has passed since the last rain was heard
> Above the ants and lizards
> Now the sun burns endlessly
> The fruit paints its mouth
> The pores in the earth open slowly
> And beside the water that drips in syllables
> A huge plant gazes into the eye of the sun.

In another passage, an abrupt change in rhythm, a repeated phrase, suddenly turns the description of a familiar setting into a cry of ecstasy:

> The images of the Resurrection
> On walls that the pine-trees scratched with their fingers
> This whitewash that carries the noonday on its back
> And the cicadas, the cicadas in the ears of the trees.

The First Sun appeared during the occupation and for some time now has been out of print. Elytis published one more poem at the conclusion of the war, a long and substantial elegy on a hero of the Albanian campaign, then remained silent for thirteen years, that is, until the publication in 1958 of excerpts from a work called "Worthy is it" (the complete text appeared in a volume with that title published in 1959), and in 1960 of a short volume entitled *Six and One Regrets for the Sky*, from which we have chosen "The Autopsy" and "Beauty and the Illiterate." This long silence, now fortunately broken, was symptomatic of the general lethargy in Greek letters following the occupation. Another extremely talented contemporary, Nikos Gatsos (b. 1912) suffered the same fate, without any reprieve so far. Along with Seferis and Elytis, Gatsos belonged to the group that made *Ta Nea Grammata* prosper in the late thirties. He published a single volume of verse in 1943, *Amorgos,* then became silent (except for a number of translations, including a highly praised version of Lorca's *Blood Wedding*). But his single volume of verse was a startling contribution to contemporary Greek poetry: it was more impressive in quality than any first volume of poems since Seferis's *Turning Point,* published twelve years earlier. Especially exciting was the toughness of the poet's sensibility and the vitality of his diction, which was a fusion of the traditional and the colloquial. Lines such as the following (only a vague approximation in translation) offered not only a new voice but a new possibility for extending the permissible language of poetry:

> In the griever's courtyard no sun rises
> Only worms appear to mock the stars
> Only horses sprout upon the ant hills
> And bats eat birds and cast off sperm.
>
> In the griever's courtyard night never sets
> Only the foliage vomits forth a river of tears
> When the devil passes by to mount the dogs
> And the crows swim in a well of blood.

In the griever's courtyard the eye has gone dry
The brain has frozen and the heart turned to stone
Frog-flesh hangs from the spider's teeth
Hungry locusts scream at the vampire's feet.

This violence of language is ultimately tempered by a lyricism reminiscent of Elytis: "It was the face of May, the moon's whiteness/A step light as a tremor on the meadow/A kiss of the foam-trimmed sea." And the fanciful image, engendered once again by French surrealism, is offered occasionally as a counterpoint to harsher matter: we find, for example, "the snow-covered meadows of the moon," and "the kerchief of some evening" and "the ready embrace of the wounded sea." In fact, the defining characteristic of this verse—the characteristic that establishes its originality—is an ever-present tension between the violent and the lyrical, the harsh and the tender, the crude and the beautiful: in specific images, in the juxtaposition of lines, in the structure of whole poems. The passage quoted above, for example, gives us worms mocking stars, bats eating birds, foliage vomiting forth tears, a heart turned to stone; and all of this is juxtaposed with a quiet ending. The second poem in this selection, "They Say the Mountains Tremble," offers a similar series of oppositions: two small cyclamens kissing in the mud, an eagle building its nest "within your eyes," a penguin's tear falling in the frozen wilderness, the knife of some sorrow penetrating the cheek of hope, brigands singing in aromatic groves. The opening of the poem is typically violent:

They say the mountains tremble and the fir-trees rage
When night gnaws the tile-pins to let in the kallikantzari
When hell gulps down the torrents' foaming toil
Or when the hair of the pepper tree becomes the north-wind's
      plaything.

In contrast, the ending is again quiet, almost reverential (a mood reinforced by the allusion to the Eucharist):

> Enough to find a sharp sickle and a plough in a joyful hand
> Enough if a little wheat flowers for the feasts,
> A little wine for remembrance, a little water for the dust.

The tension between contraries carries over into the poet's attitude towards experience. In this poem it is that between despair and hope, cynicism and expectation (especially plausible tensions when one remembers that the poem was written during the Occupation):

> But here on this damp bank there is one way only
> One deceptive way and you must take it
> You must plunge into blood before time forestalls you,
> Cross over opposite to find your companions again
> Flowers birds deer
> To find another sea, another tenderness,
> To take Achilles' horses by the reins
> Instead of sitting dumb scolding the river
> Stoning the river like the mother of Kitso
> Because you too will be lost and your beauty will have aged.

The speaker's bravado hides a bitterness, a bitterness against decay and dying youth (the earlier allusion to Heraclitus is to the point). His hope of crossing to "another sea, another tenderness" is undercut by this bitterness: the way over is deceptive, and the need to take it is made imperative by the certainty of old age and death. The attitude here recalls the longing for a lost paradise in Seferis's poetry—the references to companions, to another sea, to the classical figure reinforce this—but in Gatsos the tone is more stark, and the longing is reduced to its barest elements, the little most necessary to sustain body and soul: wheat, wine, and water.

. . .

26

INTRODUCTION

These, then, are the six poets who have spoken most forcefully in contemporary Greek verse. Since each has his individuality and his specific interest, any generalization that includes all of them, that attempts to define the group as a whole, must be regarded with some suspicion. It can be safely said, however, that the one thing which most clearly distinguishes modern Greek poetry from that of other Western countries and which gives the contemporary movement a certain unity is the ardent consciousness that these poets share of being Greek; each projects his personal vision in terms of what that word most clearly designates for him: a mythology, a history, a landscape, a state of mind—sometimes all four of these. There is no contemporary verse more intensely local in the broadest meaning of the term, no verse that gives a more precise sense of a nation's present experience. There is also no verse more conscious of its heritage. The expression of the personal in terms of the historical, the translation of the subjective into the more objective, always characteristic of these poets, is very much in keeping with the method and spirit of their ancient Greek and Byzantine ancestors. Both in its individual representatives and as a whole the poetry of modern Greece is thus the latest expression of a long and noble tradition, a tradition in which it is sufficiently accomplished to sing without embarrassment and without presumption.

Notes are provided on pages 177–84 in explanation of the words or lines which have been marked with a (*) in the ensuing poems.

Κ.Π. Καβάφης

I   C.P.CAVAFY

Waiting for the Barbarians

What are we waiting for, gathered in the market-place?

    The barbarians are to arrive today.

Why so little activity in the Senate?
Why do the Senators sit there without legislating?

    Because the barbarians will arrive today.
    Why should the Senators bother with laws now?
    The barbarians, when they come, will do the law-making.

Why has our emperor risen so early,
and why does he sit at the largest gate of the city
on the throne, in state, wearing the crown?

    Because the barbarians will arrive today.
    And the emperor is waiting to receive
    their leader. He has even prepared
    a parchment for him. There
    he has given him many titles and names.

Why did our two consuls and our praetors go out
today in the scarlet, the embroidered, togas?
Why did they wear bracelets with so many amethysts,
and rings with brilliant sparkling emeralds?
Why today do they carry precious staves
splendidly inlaid with silver and gold?

    Because the barbarians will arrive today;
    and such things dazzle barbarians.

And why don't the worthy orators come as always
to make their speeches, say what they have to say?

    Because the barbarians will arrive today;
    and they are bored by eloquence and public speaking.

What does this sudden uneasiness mean,
and this confusion? (How grave the faces have become!)
Why are the streets and squares rapidly emptying,
and why is everyone going back home so lost in thought?

    Because it is night and the barbarians have not come.
    And some men have arrived from the frontiers
    and they say that there are no barbarians any longer.

And now, what will become of us without barbarians?
Those people were a kind of solution.

C. P. CAVAFY

The City

You said: "I shall go to another land, go to another sea.
Another town shall be found better than this one.
Ill-starred and vain is all I have ever done,
and my heart—like a dead body—within me is entombed.
For how long is my mind to this marasmus doomed?
Wherever I turn my eyes, if I gaze no matter where,
the black ruins of my life I see, here,
where so many years have I spent, destroyed, wasted utterly."

New places you will not find, you will not find another sea.
The city will follow you. And you will haunt always
the same streets, in the same suburbs pass your days,
in these very houses finally grow white.
Always you will reach this city. Hold no hope of flight—
for you there is no ship, no road anywhere.
As you have destroyed your life here
in this corner, so in the whole world have you wrecked it utterly.

The God Abandons Antony *

When suddenly at the midnight hour you hear
an invisible company pass
with exquisite music, voices—
do not lament your luck that now gives out, your work
that has failed, schemes of your life
all proved to be false—do not lament these uselessly.
Like one for long prepared, like a courageous man,
say good-bye to her, to the Alexandria who is leaving.
Above all, do not deceive yourself, do not say
it was a dream, your hearing was mistaken:
do not condescend to such vain hopes as these.
Like one for long prepared, like a courageous man,
as it becomes you who have had the honour of such a city,
go firmly to the window
and listen, with feeling but not
with a coward's supplication and complaint—
listen as the final enjoyment to the music,
to the exquisite instruments of the mysterious company,
and say good-bye to her, to the Alexandria you are losing.

Things that are Dangerous

Said Myrtias (a Syrian student
at Alexandria, in the reign
of the Emperor Constans and the Emperor Constantius;
in part a heathen, in part christianized):
"Fortified with theory and with study,
I shall not coward-like fear my passions;
I shall give my body to voluptuousness,
to the dreamt-of pleasures,
to the most audacious erotic desires,
to the violent lasciviousness of the blood, without
the slightest fear, because when I wish—
and I shall have the will-power, fortified
as I shall be with theory and with study—
at critical moments I shall find again
my spirit, as before, ascetic."

Ithaka

When you set out for Ithaka
ask that your way be long,
full of adventure, full of instruction.
The Laistrygonians and the Cyclops,
angry Poseidon—do not fear them:
such as these you will never find
as long as your thought is lofty, as long as a rare
emotion touch your spirit and your body.
The Laistrygonians and the Cyclops,
angry Poseidon—you will not meet them
unless you carry them in your soul,
unless your soul raise them up before you.

Ask that your way be long.
At many a summer dawn to enter
—with what gratitude, what joy—
ports seen for the first time;
to stop at Phoenician trading centres,
and to buy good merchandise,
mother of pearl and coral, amber and ebony,
and sensuous perfumes of every kind,
sensuous perfumes as lavishly as you can;
to visit many Egyptian cities,
to gather stores of knowledge from the learnéd.
Have Ithaka always in your mind.
Your arrival there is what you are destined for.
But do not in the least hurry the journey.
Better that it last for years,
so that when you reach the island you are old,
rich with all you have gained on the way,

not expecting Ithaka to give you wealth.
Ithaka gave you the splendid journey.
Without her you would not have set out.
She hasn't anything else to give you.

And if you find her poor, Ithaka has not deceived you.
So wise have you become, of such experience,
that already you will have understood what these Ithakas mean.

Philhellene *

Be sure the engraving is done artistically.
The expression grave and dignified.
The crown preferably narrow:
I do not care for the broad Parthian type.
The inscription, as usual, in Greek:
not exaggerated, not pompous—
one doesn't want it misunderstood by the proconsul
who is always nosing things out and reporting to Rome—
and yet of course honorific.
Something most choice on the other side:
some discus-thrower, young, beautiful.
Above all I recommend you see to it
(Sithaspes, in God's name, don't let it be forgotten)
that after the King and the Saviour
there be engraved in elegant characters: Philhellene.
And now do not start your facetiousness,
your "Where are the Greeks?" and "What hellenism
here behind Zagros, out beyond Phraata?"
Since so many others more barbarian than ourselves
inscribe it, we shall inscribe it too.
And, moreover, do not forget that sometimes
sophists come to us from Syria,
and versifiers, and other such triflers.
Thus we are not, I trust, un-hellenic.

Theodotus

If you are among the truly select,
watch how you obtain your dominance.
However greatly you are glorified, however much
the states proclaim your achievements
in Italy and in Thessaly,
whatever honours
your admirers in Rome decree for you,
neither your joy, nor the triumph will remain,
nor superior—superior indeed!—will you feel,
when, in Alexandria, Theodotus brings you
upon a blood-stained platter
the wretched Pompey's head.*

And do not be certain that in your life
restricted, regulated, and prosaic,
such spectacular and dreadful things do not take place.
Perhaps at this moment into some neighbour's
well-ordered house there goes—
invisible, unsubstantial—Theodotus,
bringing exactly such a frightful head.

Manuel Comnenos *

The Emperor Manuel Comnenos
one sad September day
felt himself close to death. The astrologers
(salaried) of the court insisted
that he still had many more years to live.
While however they were talking, he
remembers ancient pious custom,
and from the monastic cells he orders
ecclesiastical vestments to be brought,
and he wears them, and is glad that he shows
the modest aspect of a priest or a monk.

Fortunate all those who believe,
and like the Emperor Manuel end their lives
clothed so modestly according to their faith.

One of Their Gods

When one of them passed through the market
of Seleukeia, at about the hour of dusk,
like a tall youth of perfect beauty,
with the joy of the inviolate in his eyes,
with his black and perfumed hair,
the passers-by would gaze at him,
and one would ask the other if he knew him,
and if he were a Greek from Syria, or a stranger.
But some who looked with greater care
would understand and move to one side;
and while he was lost beneath the colonnade,
among the shadows and the lights of evening,
going towards the quarter that lives
only at night, with orgies and debauchery,
with every kind of drunkenness and lust,
they would wonder which of Them it could be,
and for what suspicious pleasure
he had come down into the streets of Seleukeia
from the Venerated, Most-Honoured Mansions.

The Respite of Nero

He was not worried, Nero, when he heard
the pronouncement of the Delphic Oracle:
"Beware the seventy-third year."
Time still to rejoice.
He is thirty. Most ample
the period which the god bestows
for him to deal with future dangers.

Now, a little tired, he will return to Rome,
but splendidly tired after that journey
which was day after day of enjoyment—
theatres, garden-parties, gymnasiums. . . .
Evenings in the cities of Achaia. . . .
Ah, the delight above all of naked bodies. . . .

So Nero. And in Spain Galba
secretly gathers his army and drills it—
Galba, the old man in his seventy-third year.*

Aimilianos Monae, Alexandrian
(A.D. 628–655)

With words, countenance, and manners
I will make an excellent suit of armour;
and thus I shall face wicked men
without fear and without weakness.

They will want to injure me. But no one will know,
of all those who come near me,
where my wounds lie, my vulnerable places,
beneath the falsehoods that will cover me.

Boasting words of Aimilianos Monae.
One wonders if he ever made that suit of armour.
In any case he did not wear it long.
At the age of twenty-seven, he died in Sicily.

Of Demetrius Soter

(187–150 B.C.) *

His every expectation turned out wrong!

He had imagined performing famous deeds,
to end the humiliation that since the battle
of Magnesia had oppressed his fatherland,
to make Syria again a powerful state,
with her armies, her fleets,
her big fortresses, her wealth.

He suffered, he became bitter at Rome
when he felt in the conversations of his friends,
the youth of the great families,
with all the delicacy and politeness
that they showed to him, to the son
of King Seleukos Philopater—
when he felt that none the less there was always
a secret contempt for the hellenizing dynasties:
that they are fallen, are not fit for anything serious,
quite unsuited for the leadership of peoples.
He withdrew alone, and he became indignant, and he swore
that it would not be at all as they imagined;
why, he has will-power;
he will struggle, he will achieve, he will exalt.
If he could only find a way of getting to the East,
succeed in escaping from Italy—
and all this strength he has
within his soul, all this energy
he will communicate to the people.

Ah, only to find himself in Syria!
So young he left his country
he scarcely remembers her appearance.
But in his thoughts he has conceived her always
as something holy to be approached with reverence,
as the sight of a lovely place, as the vision
of Greek cities and Greek ports.

And now?
     Now desperation and sorrow.

They were right, the young men in Rome.
It is not possible for them to endure, the dynasties
resulting from the Occupation of the Macedonians.

No matter: he himself has striven,
he has struggled as much as he could.
And in his black disillusion
one thing only he prides himself on still:
that, even in his failure,
he presents to the world the same indomitable courage.

The rest: they were dreams and vanities.
This Syria: it almost does not seem to be his country;
this Syria is the land of Heracleides and of Balas.

Darius

The poet Phernazis is composing
the important part of his epic poem:
how Darius, son of Hystaspes,
took over the kingdom of the Persians. (From him
descends our glorious king,
Mithridates, Dionysus and Eupator).* But here
philosophy is needed: he has to analyse
the feelings Darius must have had:
arrogance perhaps and intoxication? But no—more likely
a certain understanding of the vanity of greatness.
Deeply the poet ponders the matter.

But his servant, running in,
interrupts him and announces most significant news.
The war with the Romans has begun.
Most of our army has crossed the borders.

The poet is dumbfounded. What a calamity!
How can our glorious king,
Mithridates, Dionysus and Eupater,
concern himself now with Greek poems!
In the middle of a war—imagine, Greek poems!

Phernazis frets. What bad luck!
Just when he was certain with his "Darius"
to distinguish himself, and to confound
once and for all his envious critics.
What a postponement, what a postponement of his plans.

And if it were only a postponement—good enough.
But let us see whether we are safe

in Amisus. It is not a city fortified exceptionally well.
The Romans are the most frightful enemies.
Are we, the Cappadocians, able to cope
with them? Could it be possible?
Are we to measure ourselves with the legions?
Great gods, protectors of Asia, help us.

But in all his agitation and misfortune
insistently the poetical idea comes and goes—
the most likely of course is arrogance and intoxication:
arrogance and intoxication must Darius have felt.

An Exiled Byzantine Nobleman
Versifying

The frivolous let them call me frivolous.
To serious matters I was always
most attentive. And I will insist
that no one knows better than myself
the Holy Fathers or the Scriptures, or the Canons of the Synods.
In every one of his doubts, in every
ecclesiastical difficulty, Botaneiatis
consulted me, me first of all.
But exiled here (let her beware, the malicious
Irene Doukaina),* and incredibly bored,
it is not altogether out of place to amuse myself
making six-line and eight-line verses—
to amuse myself with the mythology
of Hermes and Apollo and Dionysus,
or the heroes of Thessaly and the Peloponnese;
and to compose correct iambics,
such as—if you will allow me to say so—the learnéd
at Constantinople do not know how to compose.
This correctness is, probably, the cause of their reproach.

C. P. CAVAFY

The Melancholy of Jason Kleander
Poet in Commagene, A.D. 595

The ageing of my body and my beauty
is a wound from a terrible knife.
I lack all resistance.
Towards you I turn, O Art of Poetry,
who somehow know about drugs:
attempts to numb the pain, in Imagination and Word.

It is a wound from a terrible knife.
Bring your drugs, O Art of Poetry,
which ease the wound for a little while at least.

From the School of the Renowned
Philosopher

For two years he was a pupil of Ammonius Sakkas; *
but he was bored by both the philosophy and Sakkas.

Afterwards he went into politics.
But he gave them up. The Prefect was a fool,
and his entourage solemn and sombre blockheads:
their Greek disgusting, the idiots.

His curiosity was attracted
a little by the Church: to be baptised
and to pass as a Christian. But quickly
he changed his mind. He would, doubtless, quarrel
with his parents, ostentatious pagans;
and they at once would stop—a frightful thing—
their most generous allowance.

He had however to do something. He began to haunt
the corrupt houses of Alexandria,
every secret den of debauchery.

Fortune had been kind to him in this:
she had given him a figure handsome to the extreme.
And he enjoyed the divine gift.

At least for ten years yet
would his beauty last. Afterwards—
perhaps he will go again to Sakkas.
Or if in the meantime the old man has died,
he will go to another philosopher or sophist:
someone suitable is always to be found.

Or in the end possibly he will return
even to politics—laudably remembering
the traditions of his family,
duty towards the country, and other such pomposities.

Julian and the Antiochians *

"Neither the letter CHI, they say, nor the letter
KAPPA had ever harmed the city. . . . We, finding interpreters . . . were taught that these are
the initial letters of names, the first of 'Christ'
and the second of 'Konstantios.' "
Julian's *Misopogon* (The Beard-hater)

Was it ever possible for them to renounce
their beautiful way of life; the variety
of their habitual amusements; the brilliance
of their theatre which consummated a union between Art
and the erotic tendencies of the flesh!

Immoral to a degree—and probably to more than a de-
    gree—
they were. But they had the satisfaction that their life
was the much talked of life of Antioch,
the delectable, the absolutely elegant.

To give up all this in order to attend, indeed, to what?

To his vapourings about the false goods;
his tedious self-advertisement;
his childish fear of the theatre;
his graceless prudery; his ludicrous beard.

O certainly they preferred the CHI,
certainly they preferred the KAPPA—a hundred times.

C. P. CAVAFY

A Great Procession of Priests and Laymen

A procession of priests and laymen,
each walk of life represented,
passes through streets, through squares, and through
          gates
of the famous city of Antioch.
At the head of the great imposing procession
a beautiful white-clad youth is holding
with upraised hands the Cross,
our strength and our hope, the holy Cross.
The pagans, before so thoroughly arrogant,
but submissive now, and cowards, quickly
move away from the procession.
Far from us, far from us let them remain for ever
(as long as they do not renounce their error). The holy
          Cross
goes forward. Into ever quarter
where Christians live with reverence for God
it brings consolation and joy:
they come out, the pious, to the doors of their houses
and full of exultation they worship it—
the strength, the salvation of the universe, the Cross.

This is an annual Christian festival.
But today, observe, it takes place more splendidly.
The empire is delivered at last.
The most depraved, the appalling
Julian reigns no longer.

For the most pious Jovian let our prayers be given.*

In a Large Greek Colony, 200 B.C.

That things in the Colony do not proceed as they should
no one can doubt any longer,
and although, in spite of everything, we do go forward,
perhaps, as not a few are thinking, the time has come
to introduce a Political Reformer.

But the objection and the difficulty is
that they make an enormous fuss
about everything, these
reformers. (It would be a blessing
if they were never needed). Whatever it is,
even the smallest detail, they question and investigate,
and at once radical reforms enter their heads
demanding to be executed without delay.

Also they have a liking for sacrifice:
RID YOURSELF OF THAT POSSESSION;
YOUR OWNERSHIP IS DANGEROUS:
EXACTLY SUCH POSSESSIONS DAMAGE COLONIES.
RID YOURSELF OF THAT INCOME,
AND OF THE OTHER CONNECTED WITH IT,
AND OF THIS THIRD, AS A NATURAL CONSEQUENCE;
THEY ARE ESSENTIAL, BUT WHAT CAN ONE DO?
THEY CREATE AN INJURIOUS RESPONSIBILITY FOR YOU.

And as they extend their investigation
they discover endless superfluities, and these they seek to
        remove:
things which are however renounced with difficulty.
And when, with luck, the business is completed,
and every detail is defined and circumscribed,

they retire, taking also the wages due to them,
allowing us to see whatever still remains, after
such effective surgery.

Perhaps the moment has not yet arrived.
Let us not hurry: speed is a dangerous thing.
Untimely measures bring repentance.
Certainly, and unhappily, many things are wrong in the
        Colony.
But is there anything human without imperfection?
And after all, look, we do go forward.

In Sparta *

He did not know, the king Kleomenes, he did not dare—
he did not know how to tell his mother
of such a condition: that Ptolemy had demanded,
to guarantee their treaty, that she be sent
to Egypt and that she be held there:
a very humiliating, improper thing.
And every time he was about to tell her, he hesitated.
And every time he began to speak, he stopped.

But the wonderful woman understood him
(she had heard rumours already concerning it),
and she encouraged him to explain.
And she laughed; and she said of course she would go.
And she even rejoiced that she was able
in her old age to be useful to Sparta still.

As for the humiliation—it did not interest her.
The spirit of Sparta certainly was beyond
the comprehension of an upstart like the Lagides;
therefore his demand could not in fact
humiliate an Illustrious Woman like herself:
mother of a Spartan king.

Myris: Alexandria, A.D. 340

When I learnt of the tragedy, that Myris was dead,
I went to his house, although I avoid
going into the houses of Christians,
especially at times of mourning or festivity.

I stood in the corridor. I did not wish
to go further inside, because I perceived
that the relatives of the dead regarded me
with evident surprise and displeasure.

They had him in a large room
of which from the corner where I stood
I could see a little: all precious carpets,
and vessels of silver and gold.

I stood and wept in a corner of the corridor.
And I thought how our gatherings and our excursions
would not be worthwhile any longer without Myris;
and I thought how I would no longer see him
at our beautiful and indecent all-night sessions
enjoying himself, and laughing, and reciting verses
with his perfect feel for Greek rhythm;
and I thought how I had lost for ever
his beauty, how I had lost for ever
the young man I had worshipped so madly.

Some old women, close to me, were speaking softly
of the last day that he lived—
on his lips continually the name of Christ,
in his hand he held a cross.
And then four Christian priests

came into the room, and said prayers
fervently, and orisons to Jesus,
or to Mary (I do not know their religion well).

We had known, of course, that Myris was a Christian.
From the first moment we had known it, when
the year before last he had joined our company.
But he lived exactly as we did.
Of all of us most given to pleasure;
scattering his money lavishly on amusements.
Indifferent to the world's esteem,
he threw himself eagerly into the street-fights
when at night our band happened to meet
a rival band.
He never spoke of his religion.
And once we even told him
that we would take him with us to the Serapion.
But it was as if it displeased him,
this joke of ours: I remember now.
Ah, and two other times now come to my mind.
When we made libations to Poseidon,
he drew himself back from our circle, and looked else-
        where
When one of us enthusiastically said:
"Let our company be under
the favour and the protection of the great,
 of the all-beautiful Apollo"—Myris whispered
(the others did not hear) "with the exception of myself."

The Christian priests with loud voices
were praying for the young man's soul.
I noticed with how much diligence
and with what intensive care
for the forms of their religion, they were preparing
everything for the Christian funeral.

And suddenly an odd sensation
came to me. I felt obscurely
as if Myris were going from me:
I felt that he, a Christian, had united
with his own people, and that I was becoming
a stranger, a complete stranger; I even felt
a doubt approaching: that I had been deceived
by my passion, and had always been a stranger to him.
I threw myself out of their frightful house,
I fled quickly before it was seized, before it was altered
by their Christianity, the memory of Myris.

To Have Taken Care

I have become almost a vagabond and penniless.
This fatal city, Antioch,
has devoured all my money:
this fatal city with its extravagant life.

But I am young and in excellent health.
Prodigious master of Greek
(Aristotle, Plato, I know them through and through,
whatever orator, poet, or whatever else you mention).
Of military affairs I am not ignorant,
and I have friends among the senior regular officers.
I have a certain knowledge also of administrative matters.
In Alexandria I stayed six months, last year;
something I know (and this is useful) about what goes on
        there:
the corruption, and the dirt, and the rest of it.

So I believe I am completely
qualified to serve this country,
my beloved fatherland, Syria.

In whatever job they put me I shall endeavour
to be useful to the country. That is my purpose.
But again, if they hinder me with their systems—
we know them, these smart ones: do we have to discuss
        it?—
if they hinder me it is not my fault.

I will address myself to Zabinas first,
and if that idiot doesn't appreciate me,
I shall go to his rival, Grypos.

And if that imbecile doesn't appoint me,
I shall go at once to Hyrcanus.*

In any case one of the three will want me.

And my conscience is quiet
about my indifference to the choice:
the three of them damage Syria to the same extent.

But, a ruined man, it is not my fault.
I am only trying, poor devil, to get on my feet.
The almighty gods ought to have taken care
to create a fourth, an honest man.
Gladly would I have gone along with him.

In the Outskirts of Antioch *

We were astonished in Antioch when we heard
about the new activities of Julian.

Apollo explained things to him, at Daphne!
He did not wish to give an oracle (as though we cared!),
he did not intend to speak prophetically, unless first
his temple at Daphne were cleansed.
The neighbouring dead, he declared, annoyed him.

Many tombs are to be found at Daphne.
One of those there buried
was the wonderful, the holy, the triumphant
martyr Babylas, the glory of our church.

It was him the false god hinted at, him he feared.
As long as he felt him close he did not dare
to give his oracle: not a whisper.
(The false gods are terrified of our martyrs).

The unholy Julian rolled up his sleeves,
became angry and shouted: "Raise him, carry him out,
take him away immediately, this Babylas.
Do you hear there? Apollo is annoyed.
Raise him, seize him at once,
dig him out, dispose of him where you like.
Take him away, expel him. Is this a game?
Apollo said the temple is to be cleansed."

We took it, we carried it, the holy relic, elsewhere.
We took it, we carried it, in love and in honour.
And excellently indeed has the temple prospered!

No time had elapsed when a colossal fire
flared up; a terrible fire;
and both the temple and Apollo were burnt.

Ashes the idol; sweepings, with the rubbish.

Julian exploded, and he spread it round—
what else could he do?—that we, the Christians,
had set the fire. Let him say so.
It hasn't been proved. Let him say so.
The essential thing is—that he exploded.

Ἄγγελος Σικελιανός

II ANGHELOS
SIKELIANOS

The Return

Holy sleep, and lion-like,
of the return, on the vast
stretch of sand.
In my heart the eyelids closed,
and light, like a sun, within me.

Sea-sound floods my veins,
above me the sun
like a mill-wheel grinds,
the wind beats wide wings;
unseen the axle throbs;
my deep breath is not heard,
and the sea, as on the sand,
calms and spreads within me.

Into high-domed waves
the boundless caress raises it;
the cool seaweed
freshens the bowels;
the foam's lucid spindrift
breaks into spray upon the pebbles;
beyond, where the cicadas call full-voiced,
the leaves' rustle ceases.

A sound comes from far;
and suddenly,
as a sail when the yard-arm breaks,
beats; it is the wind that approaches,
it is the sun that sets before my eyes
and, chaste, I open my kindred eyelids
to its all-white look.

I leap up. My lightness
is equal to my strength.
Cool my forehead glows,
in the sunset my body
stirs deeply like spring.
I gaze about me: the Ionian sea,
and my delivered land!

The Horses of Achilles

O asphodel plain, beside you
two neighing horses
passed at a gallop . . .
Their backs shone like a wave;
they rose up from the sea,
they tore the desolate sand,
with necks outstretched, stallions,
towering, white with foam . . .
In their eyes the lightning
smouldered secretly; and waves,
they sank again into the wave,
foam in the ocean's foam,
and vanished. And I knew
those steeds, of which the one,
prophetic, assumed a human voice.
The hero held the reins;
he struck, and thrust forward
his godlike youth . . .

Sacred steeds, fate
inviolate has kept you, fixing
to your pitch-black foreheads
against the profane eye
a large and pure-white talisman.

The First Rain

We leaned from the open window.
All was one with our mood.
Sulphur-pale, the clouds
made field and vineyard dark,
with secret turbulence
wind moaned in the trees,
and the quick swallow went
breasting across the grass.
Then suddenly the thunder
broke, and tore the sky,
and dancing came the rain.
The dust leapt in the air.
We, as our nostrils felt
the teeming earth-smell, held
our lips open, to let it
water deep in the breast.
Then, side by side, our faces
as mullen and as the olive
already wet with rain:
"What smell," we asked, "is this,
that bee-like rends the air?
From balsam, pine, acanthus,
osier or the thyme?"
So was it, that, as I breathed,
sweetness filled my mouth,
I stood, a lyre, caressed
by its profusion, till,
meeting again your gaze,
blood clamoured in every vein.
I bent above the vine,
leaf-shuddering, to drink

its honey and its flower;
nor could I—my mind a dense
grape-cluster, bramble-caught the breath—
single those smells, but reaped
and gathered all, and all
drank as one does from fate
sorrow or sudden joy;
I drank them down, and when
I touched your waist, my blood
like the nightingale sang out
and ran like all the waters.

Vernal

Fiery, mirthful, warm, the moon looked forth
    above the vineyards;
and still the sun burnt the bushes, setting
    in a double stillness.

The heavy grass up on the windless height
    sweated its angry sap,
and from among the youthful vines, which climbed
    the terraced slope,

the vine-keepers whistled and waved, the robins
    hovered at the side,
and now across the moon the heat had spread
    a fine, filmy mantle . . .

In the corn, in line the one behind the other,
    three oxen alone
ascended the mountain slope, their pendant
    dewlaps swaying.

The slender hound, his muzzle to the earth,
    with rapid footsteps
in the evening quietness leapt from rock to rock,
    searching for my tracks.

And at the house ahead, beneath the unripe vine,
    a ready table
awaited me, lit—a lamp hung out before it—
    by the evening star . . .

There, the master's daughter brought me wheaten bread,
    water cold, and honey-comb;

she had from vigour round her marble throat
    a circle like a dove,

and in her glance, as in the evening light, there burnt
    virginity's lucid flame,
and through the tight dress that covered her firm breasts
    the nipple stood out clearly;

and in two braids her plaited hair was raised
    above her forehead,
braids like a ship's cable which I could not
    have clasped with a single hand.

The dog which had been roused on the steep footpaths
    now stood there, panting,
and motionless on his front legs regarded me, waiting
    my fist between the eyes.

There, as I heard the nightingale, and ate
    fruit from the dish before me,
I had the taste of wheat upon my palate,
    of honey, and of song.

As in a glass hive within me moved my soul,
    a joyful bee-swarm,
that secretly increasing seeks to loosen on the trees
    its grape-like cluster.

And I felt the earth as crystal beneath my feet,
    the soil transparent,
for the strong and peaceful body of young plane-trees
    rose up about me.

There they opened their old wine for me, smelling
    rich in the porous jar,

as mountain scents when the cool night dew
    falls on the bushes . . .

Fiery, mirthful, warm, there my heart consented
    to repose a while,
in sheets made fragrant by the herbs, azure
    by the washing blue. . . .

ANGHELOS SIKELIANOS

From The Village Wedding

Tethered the horses,
let them wait in the paved courtyard
which, while the guests gather,
echoes with their hooves;

And crowded suddenly
croup to croup, let the mules
rise on their hind legs for room;

while on their backs
spread with the woven covers
the wedding guests
adorned with silk and gold
riding side-saddle
gently shake the reins
to set out together
(and it is a clear day and blue, Sunday,
and from the village depths
the sound of the new bell spills
as the complaining call
of a cow
swollen with too much milk.

And the whole village has emptied

into the sunlit threshing-floor
before the church!)

But in the village opposite
let the diaphanous silence grow!

The bride sits
on a low polished stool,
she gazes neither to the right nor to the left,

while her handmaids,
standing behind her back,
part her hair in the middle
on the top of her head,
and when they have combed it through,
and have shaken it out into the air this way and
        that,
powerfully,
with three fingers separating
the soft treasure,
they begin with gentle hands
to braid the plaits
like slings
the one on top of the other! . . .

(But from the bride, unmoving, all round,
covered now with the delicate head-dress,
let the crystal silence pour.

And virginal let the thought flow
as on deep-grassy slopes
in the windless sun
the flowering of the wild pear-tree).

In your veil do you listen,
silent, God-quickened heart?

There it is, the first tread of the mules
kicking the stones as they come!

But riding on horseback, leading the way, the bride-
        groom
greets all creation as his dowry!

His body drinks the sun,
drinks as a hot beach of fine sand
the ever-renewing foam! . . .

His strength is tilled, and closes
as the soil after the corn!

And at last now:
as he alights on the threshold of the house,
facing the bride,

his heart suddenly stills!

(O depth and silence of Virginity!)

Like a spring cloud let her now spread
the wedding-veil tenderly.

Like a spring shower
let the white rice be thrown!
In the light of day
let the flames of the candles
like fine gold
rise from their naked wicks!

And now at last
the pigeon flies
for the bridegroom's house . . .

And there, far off, is the new home!

With honey the bridegroom's mother
anoints the threshold,

on the lintel she breaks the pomegranate
before the bride enters.*

As the rolled mattress opens,
let the whole room smell of fruit!

Let the veil be thrown off
as the blossom of an almond-tree!

Let the bed seem of marble
before the souls of the newly-married!

O cool woven sheets
like the snows of March!

O mind dazed before the open altar!

Flesh chilled at first to the finger-tips!

Breath
like a lily that the north-wind has frozen!

Orange-blossom
hung in the white light of a virginal death!

As snakes from winter
from your sweet drowsiness you wake
O Virginity!

And suddenly,
in the depths of expectation,
O scent of the hive!

ANGHELOS SIKELIANOS

Sudden breath of honey
on the palate! . . .

creation of man from the beginning
in the divine Image!

From his side full-bodied joy
secretly nourished!

His hands, sunk in the loosened hair,
let him now plunge wholly
as into a heap of corn!

Let him now reap the richest field
of creative fragrance! . . .

Sparta *

"A long time now I've lain in wait for you;
even as though you were a star, my eye
has picked you out among all other men;
your countenance has satisfied my heart.

Listen. . . . Let me clasp you firmly by the hand:
thus, stallion-like, is youth made tractable. . . .
For but a single night, in my own bed,
you will lie companion to my wife.

Go. . . . She is deep-girdled and compact
in loveliness as the tall Helen was. . . .
Fill her with your young and generous seed. . . .

Clasp her to your powerful embrace
for one night only, and with a worthy son
raise before Sparta my barren, dry old age!"

Doric

Her hair upgathered thus behind the neck
as the Dorian Apollo's hair, her limbs
held shivering upon the narrow bed
in the indissoluble and heavy cloud. . . .

Artemis emptied all her arrows at her.
And if she was a virgin yet a while,
tightly like a cold honeycomb she sealed
between her virgin legs the sensual bliss. . . .

As though within the struggle of the ring
there while she lay the oil-anointed youth
upon her knelt, as might a wrestler kneel. . . .

And if he broke the repulse of her arms
it was that they now slowly, with a single cry,
might lock their limbs, and in the sweat embrace! . . .

Prayer

Naked the soul prays to You. From joy, from suffering naked;
    from pleasure
naked the soul prays to You, Creator, with alone the uncreated
    voice,

Which, before entering my flesh, on Your breast—as cicada hid-
    den in the olive—
hammered Your will into my heart, and said: "Victory, victory
    in everything!" and it was not

My speech, it was Yours, Lord. With that alone I pray to You:
    deliver to me
the secret purpose which deep and outside time I tasted, that I
    may love, that I may love

Beyond forms and creations, beyond the single pulse I close
    within me,
one now both for the living and the dead; grant me, yes, deliver-
    ance,

to know again, my God, the uncreated Eros whole within my
    breast,
to be to all, to what is near and far, as the wind's sound and
    breath. . . .

Hymn to Artemis Orthia *

O Taygetus,
bronze mountain,
ascetic you at last receive me!

O jagged range,
you closed behind me,
leaving me in solitude
as when a ram descending
from sheer cliff to stone basin
suddenly, turning to escape,
knows that it is not possible,

because the same rocks
which helped him to go down
now slip in the ascent,
untrodden,
on all sides!

In solitude you enclosed me,
in the extreme wilderness,
only to pivot on my own heel,
to look at you, huge bronze fortress!

Neither forward, nor back!
but here, on this spot,
without room to lie down or to stretch,
but here on this same spot,
upright!

O fire-giver of men,
I have not heard ascend,

from the steep precipice,
the consolation of the Oceanides!

But on all sides the rock,
the heart of earth,
the soil which at each moment gave out
a smell stronger than the ocean tempest,
sinking and playing in the waves,
ship without rudder,
my tiny breath!

And my blood throbbed in my ears,
and my eyes shot sparks,
as in the grate a new-lit fire
before bellows!

But when at last my soul, Taygetus,
rested upon your wild fragrance,

and my sorrowful heart—
which had lamented in the night
as the wood-owl
that hangs upside down from the branch,
letting the lament drip
warmly into the earth,

and as the slaughtered lamb
which they hang with its head down,
that the surplus blood run from the mouth—
when my sorrowful heart
felt suddenly in an eagle's nest
made of dry twigs,
simple and firm like the trivet,

O new-born life
that fed my untamable and silent strength,

veil of the clamour on your five peaks
where slowly the snow was thawing,

aerial waterfalls
of the full-budding oleander
on the precipice,

rising of the Dorian Apollo
before my eyes,
O harsh chiselled apparition
on the red unsoftened bronze!

O my eyes, fed at last like the lion's
in the impenetrable dark of the mountain!

deep silence, where not a breath stirs,
and my hands invisible
in the pitch-black of the damp night,

O reflections,
like bats circling in shadow,

when suddenly from Sparta
rose before me—
huge, round,
dipped in blood,
like Your shield,
Artemis Orthia—
the full moon,
and, behind, Yourself,
more than night
inflexible and silent and dark!

Your first arrows
began to shake the silence!

About my ears they whistled,
thinly aimed,
as at a mark in the darkness
which you alone saw from above!

Low laid
the twined reeds shone
with the dew of Eurotas.

Then in the red plain
the Laconian bitches howled,
their hair upright, hearing above them
the message of Your bow,
and they gnashed their teeth,
staring at the ferocious moon
which hid Your silent struggle
as behind a fire!

Prepared for death,
steadfast until I felt it from You,
I raised myself on tip-toe,
supporting You,

and as You,
who drew back the arrow to Your ear,
to find out, from the vibration
the cord made on its release,
whether it missed or found the mark,
so I to my ear brought,
one by one,
each word,
before my mouth—
which was closed, the teeth locked like a dead-
man's—

opened in a more solemn Hymn
that plumbed the Love of Earth,
the soil of my heart and of my breath,
Orthia,
to You!

"O You who, bending, feel
the muzzles of Your hounds,
which,
all together,
at the first stretching of the bow,
panting to keep up with You
as You lead the chase,
overshoot the mark,
and when You stop,
all together,
hanging their tongues out breathlessly,
circling You with joy,
scatter their hot breath on Your face!

O Orthia,
in the blind dark
the harsh white of Your eye
flashes like the wolf's teeth,
who, with lips snarling
gathers himself to spring!

With what a cry
You turn all things
suddenly
to the source of their desire and strength!

And see!
oxgoad, dogs, horses,
soil, waters

follow
in the wake of Your onrush and Your thirst!

Death a firm step
for You to tread up by!

Your hair a plaited sling,
and Your breast's steel nipple
unsoftened and dark!

You did not bend to sow the earth with corn,
but, silent, whipped
the young men until they bled,
and Your own chaste figure bending over them,
which, sweating, smelt
stronger than the wood's heart,
spurred them
to the last gasp
of the ascent,
promising to their parched throats
the only spring:
the summit!

O Orthia,
Your cupped hand ready
to collect the wounds' blood,
like that of the workman
who collects resin
from cedar or pine
cut for the purpose!

O Orthia,
with what calm alone You lead
as the peasant's wife leads
from the fields

the fiercest colt to mount the mare,
the most splendid young bull to the cow—
the virgin athlete,
resistant and submissive,
with head bent like the stallion,
to the proud maiden of Your rule.

Simple Your rule's scale:
the Dorian mode an uncaptured wall!

O Orthia,
Your command bent all,
going like a lion at the side of man,
but the secret-biting dog followed behind him,
when the virgins,
drunk from the contest
the hot afternoon
in the forests of Taygetus
like torches hidden in soot,
with submissive groan
tightening the embrace
joined fast the lips
for the tribades to relieve the weight
of the struggling virginity,

while here,
at the same time,
the chief
leads to his wife's bed
the heavy athlete,
seeing in his old mind only the bud
like the twin-star of the Dioscuri
with the lightness of Hyacinth
or the superb beauty of Nereus!

O Orthia,
You who chose as Your heart's port
the restless expanse of Your sea at Taenarum,*
which seethes,
struggles,
moans
like no other Ocean,
O when, when,
into the crawling dark of the waves
will sink and weave for ever
the enemies' dull-red blood?

O into our soul at last breathe Your shiver
more cold than the snow's wind
which sweeps suddenly—
a river of air—
whatever it finds into Your narrow gorges!

O when at last,
Huntress,
with naked foot beating the snow all night,
shall we see on the summit,
like Boreas,
the Lion
that at dawn rouses himself from sleep,

when in the light
the contest will be decided,
and the triumphant youths
will roll the opponent from the cliff-top,
and each life
in the golden light will be harvested,
as beside the sheaf the poppy
unreflecting and silent?

ANGHELOS SIKELIANOS

Draw out the pain from within us
as Hercules Cerberus from Hades,
when, spreading on the earth his belly
and with claws dragging,
the Dog followed him, inexplicable weight,
with his tail beneath his haunches,
and his eye shrinking from the Hero
as though he gazed at the Sun!

End your secret Apollo's sharp cry
O Orthia,
You who assist—
untouched and virginal—
the embrace's struggle
and the sacred moment of birth!

Bind and rivet the seed
in the heart of man!

In the womb of woman
root the male!"

The Sacred Way *

Through the new wound which fate had opened in me
it seemed the setting sun entered my heart
with the impetus of water entering suddenly
the breach in a sinking ship. . . . For again at dusk
like one long sick when first he ventures forth
to milk life from the outside world, I was
walking alone along the road which starts
from Athens, and has as its sacred destination
Eleusis. For that road always seemed to me
as the Soul's road. . . . It bore, like an enormous
river, slow ox-drawn carriages upon it, full
of sheaves or piled high with wood, and other
carriages, which quickly passed before me,
the people who were in them shadow-like.

But out beyond, as if the world were lost
and nature alone remained, hour after hour
a quietness held sway. . . . And the rock I found
rooted at one side seemed a throne
long predestined to me. And as I sat
I folded my hands upon my knees, forgetting
if I this morning had set out, or if
ages ago that self-same road had taken. . . .

But then! round the near corner into this
quietness three shadows entered. A Gypsy
came from opposite, and following him, dragged
by chains, there came two heavy-footed bears.

And then! as they came near to where I sat
the Gypsy saw me—before I had seen him well—,

drew the tambourine from off his shoulder,
beat upon it, and with his other hand
tugged the chains with force. And the two bears
rose on their hind-legs heavily. The one,
the larger (she was the mother certainly),
her head adorned with tassels of blue beads,
with a white amulet on top, rose up
suddenly enormous, as if she were
the Great Goddess's primordial image,
the Eternal Mother's, she who divinely sad,
as with time she assumed a human form,
was in her longing for her daughter called
here Demeter, in her longing for her son
elsewhere Alcmene or the Madonna.
And the small bear beside her, like a big
toy, like an innocent child, rose up as well
submissive, not guessing yet its suffering's length
nor the bitterness of slavery mirrored in
the burning eyes the mother turned upon him.

But since from weariness she was slow to dance,
the Gypsy, with a single dexterous jerk
upon the chain in the younger bear's nostril,
bloody still from the ring put in it seemed
but a few days before, suddenly made her,
as she groaned with pain, straighten up, and then,
turning her head towards her child, dance
livelily. . . .

        And I, as I watched, was drawn
outside and far from time, free from forms
closed in time, from statues and from images.
I was outside and removed from time. . . .

But nothing I saw in front of me except
the huge bear, with the blue beads on her head,

raised by the ring's wrench and her own tenderness,
sad enormous testifying symbol of
all the world, of the present and the past,
sad enormous testifying symbol of
all primaeval suffering, for which still
throughout the human centuries the soul's
tax has not been paid. . . . For the soul as yet
has been and is in Hell. . . .

And the whole time
I—slave of the world that I also am—
bowed my head as into the tambourine
I threw a single penny. . . .

But as the Gypsy
went away at last, dragging again
the two slow-footed bears behind, and vanished
in the dusk, my heart prompted me to take
once more the road which terminates among
the ruins of the Soul's temple, at Eleusis.
And, as I walked, my heart within me groaned:
"Will the time come, will the moment ever come
when both the soul of the bear and the Gypsy's soul,
and my own soul as well, which I call initiated,
shall feast together?"

And as I continued on,
night fell, and again through the same wound
which fate had opened in me, I felt darkness
entering impetuously into my heart
as water enters suddenly through the breach
of a sinking ship. . . . But as if for such a flood
my heart has thirsted, when it had sunk down
as though to drown into the pitch-black dark,

when it had sunk down to the pitch-black dark,
a murmur spread through all the air above me,
a murmur,
     and it seemed to say:
          "It will come . . ."

Unwritten

A little while before the sun had set,
as Jesus and his disciples were out walking
beyond the walls of Zion, they unexpectedly
came near the quarter where for years the town
had dumped its refuse—burnt mattresses
of the sick, broken crocks, rags, rubbish, filth.

And there, upon the highest mound, its legs
turned skyward, lay a dog's bloated carcass
which, as the crows covering it took flight
when suddenly they heard the footsteps, gave out
such stench that all the disciples, holding
their breath with their hands, as one man drew back.

But Jesus, walking calmly on alone
towards the mound, stopped short and gazed upon
the carcass so, that one of the disciples,
not able to restrain himself, cried out
to him from far: "Master, do you not sense
the terrible smell, that you stand there in that way?"

And he, his eyes not moving from the spot
at which he gazed, replied: "He with pure breath
will even in the town from which we come
breathe the terrible stench. . . . But now I marvel
with all my soul at what from this decay
there issues. . . . See how that dog's teeth are sparkling
in the sun; like hailstone, like the lily,
beyond the putrefaction, a great promise,
reflection of the Eternal, but still more
the harsh hope and lightning-flash of Justice!"

Thus He spoke; and whether the disciples
understood these words or not, together,
as He moved on, they followed once again
His silent path. . . .

        And now, how I, indeed
the least of men, do turn my mind, O Lord,
toward Your words, and on one thought intent
before You stand: Ah! grant, grant to me even
as I now walk outside the town of Zion,
and from the earth's one end until the other
all is desolation, all is rubbish,
all unburied corpses which choke up
the sacred spring of breath, within the city
or outside the city; grant, O Lord, to me
amid this frightful stench through which I pass
for one moment only Your holy calm,
so that I too, dispassionate, may pause
among this carrion and somewhere seize
with my own eyes a token, white as hailstone,
as the lily, something sparkling suddenly
deep within me, outside the putrefaction,
beyond the world's decay, like the dog's teeth
at which that evening as You gazed upon them
You, O Lord, had marvelled, a great promise,
reflection of the Eternal, but still more
the harsh hope and lightning-flash of Justice! . . .

The Suicide of Atzesivano,
Disciple of Buddha

Irreproachably Atzesivano
took the knife. And his soul
at that moment was a white pigeon . . .
And as in the night a star
falls from the skies' inmost sanctuary,
or as apple-blossom drops in the gentle wind,
so his spirit departed from his breast.

Such deaths do not go wasted . . .
For only those who love life
in its mystical first glory
can reap alone
the great harvest of their existence,
which sinks at last, with divine tranquillity!

Γιῶργος Σεφέρης

III   GEORGE SEFERIS

I

From Mythical Story *

For three years
we waited intently for the messenger
watching closely
the pines the shore and the stars.
One with the plough's blade or the keel of the ship,
we were searching to find the first seed
that the ancient drama might begin again.

We returned to our homes broken,
our limbs incapable, our mouths ruined
by the taste of rust and brine.
When we awoke we journeyed towards the north, strangers
plunged into mists by the spotless wings of swans that wounded
      us.
On winter nights the strong wind from the east maddened us,
in the summers we were lost in the agony of the day which
      could not die.

We brought back
these carved reliefs of a humble art.

3

From Mythical Story

"Remember the bath by which you were slain"
Aeschylus, *The Libation Bearers,* 491.

I awoke with this marble head in my hands
which exhausts my elbows and I do not know where to set it
     down.
It was falling into the dream as I was coming out of the dream
so our lives joined and it will be very difficult to part them.

I look at the eyes: neither open nor closed
I speak to the mouth which keeps trying to speak
I hold the cheeks which have passed beyond the skin
I have no more strength.

My hands disappear and come back to me
multilated.

4

From Mythical Story

Argonauts

And the soul,
if she is to know herself,
must look
into the soul: *
the stranger and enemy, we saw him in the mirror.

The companions were good lads: they did not complain
either at the labour or the thirst or the frost,
they had the bearing of trees and waves
which accept the wind and the rain
accept the night and the sun
without changing in the midst of change.
They were good lads, whole days
they sweated at the oar with lowered eyes
breathing in rhythm
and their blood reddened a submissive skin.
Sometimes they sang, with lowered eyes
when we passed the desolate island with the barbary figs
to the west, beyond the cape of the dogs
that bark.
If she is to know herself, they said
into the soul she must look, they said
and the oars struck the gold of the sea
in the sunset.
We passed many capes many islands the sea
leading to the other sea, gulls and seals.
Sometimes unfortunate women wept
lamenting their lost children

and others raging sought Alexander the Great
and glories buried in the depths of Asia.
We moored on shores full of night-scents
with the singing of birds, waters which left on the hands
the memory of a great happiness.
But the voyages did not end.
Their souls became one with the oars and the rowlocks
with the solemn face of the prow
with the channel made by the rudder
with the water that shattered their image.
The companions with lowered eyes
died one by one. Their oars
mark the place where they sleep by the shore.*

No one remembers them. Justice.

5

From Mythical Story

We did not know them
                it was hope deep down that said
We had known them since early childhood.
We saw them perhaps twice and then they took to the ships;
cargoes of coal, cargoes of grain, and our friends
lost forever beyond the ocean.
Dawn finds us beside the weary lamp
drawing on the paper, with great effort and awkwardly,
ships mermaids or sea-shells;
at dusk we go down to the river
because it shows us the way to the sea;
and we spend the nights in cellars that smell of tar.

Our friends have left us
                perhaps we never saw them, perhaps
we met them when sleep
still brought us close to the breathing wave
perhaps we seek them because we seek the other life
beyond the statues.

8

From Mythical Story

What do our souls seek journeying
on the decks of decayed ships
crowded with sallow women and crying infants
unable to forget themselves, either with the flying fish
or with the stars which the tips of the masts indicate,
grated by gramophone records
bound unwillingly by non-existent pilgrimages
murmuring broken thoughts from foreign tongues?

What do our souls seek journeying
on rotten, sea-borne timbers
from harbour to harbour?

Shifting broken stones, inhaling
the pine's coolness with less ease each day
swimming in the waters of this sea
and of that sea
without touch
without men
in a country which is no longer ours
nor yours

We knew that the islands were beautiful
somewhere round about here where we are groping—
a little lower or a little higher,
the slightest distance.

9
From Mythical Story

The harbour is old, I cannot wait any longer
for the friend who left for the island of pine-trees
or the friend who left for the island of plane-trees
or the friend who left for the open sea.
I caress the rusted cannons, I caress the oars
so that my body may revive and become resolute.
The sails give off the odour only
of salt from the other storm.

If I wanted to remain alone, what I sought
was solitude, not such expectation
the shattering of my soul at the horizon
these lines, these colours, this silence.

The stars of the night bring me back to the anticipation
of Odysseus awaiting the dead among the asphodels.*
When we moored here among the asphodels we wished to find
the gorge which knew Adonis wounded.

10

From Mythical Story

Our country is enclosed, all mountains
which have the low sky for a roof day and night.
We have no rivers, we have no wells, we have no springs,
only a few cisterns—and these empty—which echo and which
      we worship.
A sound stagnant, hollow, the same as our loneliness
the same as our love, the same as our bodies.
We find it strange that once we were able to build
our houses, huts, and sheepfolds.
And our marriages, the cool coronals and the fingers
become enigmas inexplicable to our soul.
How were our children born, how did they grow?

Our country is enclosed. The two black
Symplegades enclose it. When we go down *
to the harbours on Sunday to breathe
we see, alight in the sunset,
the broken timbers of voyages unfinished
bodies that no longer know how to love.

12

From Mythical Story

Bottle in the Sea

Three rocks, a few burnt pines, an abandoned chapel
and farther above
the same landscape repeated starts again;
three rocks in the shape of a gate-way, rusted,
a few burnt pines, black and yellow,
and a square hut buried in whitewash;
and farther above, the same landscape
recurs level after level
to the horizon, to the darkening sky.

Here we moored the ship to splice the broken oars
to drink water and to sleep.
The sea which embittered us is deep and unexplored
and unfolds a boundless calm.
Here among the pebbles we found a coin
and threw dice for it.
The youngest won it and disappeared.*

We set out again with our broken oars.

15

From Mythical Story

"Quid πλατανῶν opacissimus?"
Pliny, *Letters*, I, 3.

Sleep enfolded you in green leaves like a tree
you breathed like a tree in the quiet light
in the translucent spring I watched your form:
eyelids closed, eyelashes brushing the water.
In the soft grass my fingers found your fingers
I held your pulse a moment
and felt elsewhere your heart's pain.

Beneath the plane-tree, near the water, amidst the laurel
sleep removed you and scattered you
around me, near me, without my being able to touch the whole
        of you
one as you were with your silence;
seeing your shadow grow and diminish,
lose itself in the other shadows, in the other
world which released you yet held you back.

The life which they gave us to live, we lived.
Pity those who wait with such patience
lost in the black laurel beneath the heavy plane-trees
and those who speak in solitude to cisterns and wells
and drown in the voice's circles.
Pity the companion who shared our privations and our sweat,
who plunged into the sun like a crow beyond the marble ruins
without hope of enjoying our reward.

Give us, beyond sleep, serenity.

22
From Mythical Story

So very much having passed before our eyes
that our eyes in the end saw nothing but, beyond
and behind, memory like the white drape one night in an en-
    closure
where we saw strange visions, even stranger than you,
pass by and vanish in the motionless foliage of a pepper-tree;

Having known this fate of ours so well
wandering around among broken stones, three or six thousand
    years
searching in collapsed buildings which might have been our
    homes
trying to remember dates and heroic deeds:
shall we now be able?

Having been bound and scattered,
having struggled, as they said, with non-existent difficulties
lost, finding again a road full of blind regiments
sinking in marshes and in the lake of Marathon,
shall we now be able to die properly?

24

From Mythical Story

Here end the works of the sea, the works of love.
Those who will some day live here where we end—
if the blood should chance to darken in their memory and over-
       flow—
let them not forget us, the weak souls among the asphodels,*
let them turn towards Erebus the heads of the victims:*

We who had nothing will teach them peace.

GEORGE SEFERIS

The King of Asine

'Ασίνην τε . . .
Iliad, II, 560.

We looked all morning round the citadel *
starting from the shaded side, there where the sea,
green and without reflection—breast of a slain peacock—
accepted us like time without a single gap.
The veins of rock descended from high above,
twisted vines, naked, many-branched, coming alive
at the touch of water, while the eye following them
fought to escape the tiresome rocking,
losing strength continually.

On the sunny side, a long open beach
and the light striking diamonds on the large walls.
No living thing, the wild doves gone
and the king of Asine, whom we have been searching for two
      years now,
unknown, forgotten by all, even by Homer,
only one word in the *Iliad* and that uncertain,
thrown there like the gold burial mask.
You touched it, remember its sound? Hollow in the light
like a dry jar in dug earth:
the same sound that our oars make in the sea.
The king of Asine a void beneath the mask
everywhere with us everywhere with us, behind a single phrase:
"'Ασίνην τε . . . 'Ασίνην τε . . ."
                          and his children statues
and his desires the fluttering of birds, and the wind
in the interstices of his thoughts, and his ships
anchored in a vanished port:
beneath the mask a void.

Behind the large eyes the curved lips the curls
in relief on the gold cover of our being
a dark spot which you see travelling like a fish
in the dawn-like quiet of the sea:
a void everywhere with us.
And the bird that flew away last winter
with a broken wing
the shelter of life,
and the young woman who left to play
with the dogteeth of summer
and the soul which screeching sought the lower world
and the country like a large plane-leaf swept along by the tor-
        rent of the sun
with the ancient monuments and the contemporary sorrow.

And the poet lingers, looking at the stones, and asks himself
does there really exist
among these ruined lines, edges, points, hollows, and curves
does there really exist
here where one meets the path of rain, wind, and ruin
does there exist the movement of the face, shape of the tender-
        ness
of those who diminished so strangely in our lives,
those who remained the shadow of waves and thoughts bound-
        less as the sea
or perhaps, no, nothing is left but the weight
the nostalgia of the weight of a living being
there where we now remain unsubstantial, bending
like the branches of an awful willow-tree heaped in the perma-
        nence of despair
while the yellow current slowly carries down rushes uprooted
        in the mud
image of a form turned to marble by the decision of an eternal
        bitterness:
the poet a void.

Shieldbearer, the sun climbed warring,
and from the depths of the cave a startled bat
hit the light like an arrow hits a shield:
"Ἀσίνην τε Ἀσίνην τε . . .". If only that were the king of Asine
we have been searching for so carefully on this acropolis
sometimes touching with our fingers his very touch upon the
        stones.

Stratis the Mariner Among the Agapanthi

Transvaal, 14 January '42

There are no asphodels, no violets, no hyacinths;
how then can one talk with the dead?
The dead know the language of flowers only,
and so keep silent
they journey and are silent, endure and are silent,
beyond the community of dreams, beyond the community
       of dreams.*

If I start to sing I will call out
and if I call out—
the agapanthi order silence *
raising the tiny hand of a blue Arabian child
or even the footfalls of a goose in the air.

It is painful and difficult, the living are not enough for me
first because they do not speak, and then
because I have to ask the dead
in order to advance.
Otherwise I cannot: the moment I fall asleep
the companions cut the silver strings
and the flask of the winds empties.*
I fill it and it empties, I fill it and it empties;
I awaken
like a goldfish swimming
in the lightning's crevices
and the wind and the flood and the human bodies
and the agapanthi nailed like the arrows of fate
to the unquenchable earth
shaken by spasmodic nodding,

as if loaded on an ancient cart
jolting down ruined roads, over old cobblestones,
the agapanthi, asphodels of the negroes:
How can I grasp this religion?

The first thing God made is love
then comes blood
and the thirst for blood
stimulated by
the body's sperm as by salt.
The first thing God made is the long journey;
the house there is waiting
with its blue smoke
with its aged dog
waiting for the return so that it can die.
But the dead must guide me;
it is the agapanthi that hold them speechless
like the depths of the sea or the water in a glass.
And the companions remain in the palaces of Circe:
my dear Elpenor! My poor, idiotic Elpenor! *
Or don't you see them
—"Oh help us!"—
on the blackened ridge of Psara? *

An Old Man on the River Bank

Cairo, 20 June '42

And yet we must consider how we advance.
To feel is not enough, nor to think, nor to move
nor to endanger your body in an old loophole
when the scalding oil and molten lead furrow the walls.

And yet we must consider towards what we advance,
not as our pain wants it, and our hungry children
and the chasm of the companions' calling from the opposite
     shore;
nor as it is whispered by the bluish light in an improvised hospi-
     tal,
the pharmaceutic glimmer on the pillow of the youth operated
     upon at noon;
but in some other fashion, I might wish to say as
the long river that emerges from the great lakes enclosed deep
     in Africa,
which was once a god and then became a road and a benefactor,
     a judge and delta;
which is never the same, as the ancient wise men taught,
and yet remains always the same body, the same bed, and the
     same Sign,
the same orientation.

I want no more than to speak simply, to be granted this grace.
Because we have burdened song with so much music that it
     is gradually sinking
and we have adorned our art so much that its features have
     been eaten away by gold
and it is time to say our few words because tomorrow the soul
     sets sail.

GEORGE SEFERIS

If pain is human we are not human beings merely to suffer pain;
that is why I think so much these days about the great river,
this meaning which advances among herbs and greenery
and beasts that graze and drink, men who sow and harvest,
great tombs and even small habitations of the dead.
This current which goes on its way and which is not so different
      from the blood of men,
from the eyes of men when they look straight ahead without
      fear in their hearts,
without the daily tremor for trivialities or even for greater
      things;
when they look straight ahead like the traveller who is used to
      gauging his road by the stars,
not like us, the other day, gazing at the closed garden of a sleepy
      Arab house,
behind the lattices the cool garden changing shape, growing
      larger and diminishing,
we too changing, as we gazed, the shape of our desire and our
      heart,
in the drop of midday, we the patient dough of a world which
      casts us out and kneads us,
caught in the embroidered nets of a life which was complete and
      turned to dust and sank into the sands
leaving behind it only that vague dizzying sway of a tall palm-
      tree.

Stratis the Mariner on the Dead Sea

Sometimes one sees in chapels built on legendary sites the
relevant biblical description quoted in English and beneath
it:
    "THIS IS THE PLACE, GENTLEMEN!"
    (Letter of Stratis the Mariner from Jerusalem)

                                July '42

Jerusalem, ungoverned city,
Jerusalem, city of refugees.

Sometimes you see at noon
a flock of scattered black leaves
slide across the asphalt road—
Migratory birds are passing under the sun
but you don't raise your head.

Jerusalem, ungoverned city!

Unknown tongues of Babel
without relation to the grammar,
the Lives of the Saints or the Book of Psalms
which they taught you to spell out in autumn
when they tied the fishing boats to the quays;
unknown tongues glued
like burned out cigarette butts to decayed lips.

Jerusalem, city of refugees!

But their eyes all speak the same word,
not the word that became man, God forgive us,
not journeys to see new places, but
the dark train of flight where infants
are fed on dirt and the sins of their parents

and the middle-aged feel the chasm
broaden between the body,
which lags behind like a wounded camel,
and the soul with its inexhaustible courage, as they say.
It is also the ships that bear them,
standing upright like embalmed bishops
in the holds, to anchor one evening softly
in the seaweed of the deep.

Jerusalem, ungoverned city!

> To the River Jordan
> three monks brought
> a small red caique
> and moored it to the banks.
> Three from Mount Athos
> sailed for three months
> and moored to a branch,
> on the Jordan banks,
> a refugee's offering.
> they hungered three months
> they thirsted three months
> were sleepless three months
> and they came from Mount Athos
> came from Salonika
> the three enslaved monks.

Like the Dead Sea, we are all
many fathoms below the level of the Aegean.
Come with me and I will show you the place:

> In the Dead Sea
> there are no fish
> there is no seaweed
> nor any sea-urchins

there is no life.
There are no creatures
that have a belly
to suffer hunger
that nourish nerves
to suffer pain,
THIS IS THE PLACE, GENTLEMEN!

In the Dead Sea
scornfulness
is no one's ware
is no one's worry.
Heart and thought
congeal in the salt
full of bitterness
and finally join
the mineral world,
THIS IS THE PLACE, GENTLEMEN!

In the Dead Sea
enemies and friends
wife and children
other relations
go and find them.
They're in Gomorrah
down on the bottom
very happy
they don't expect
any message.
GENTLEMEN,

we continue our tour
many fathoms below the level of the Aegean.

The Last Stop

Cava dei Tirreni, 5 October '44

Few the moonlit nights that have pleased me:
the alphabet of the stars—which you spell out
as well as your fatigue at the day's end allows
and from which you discern other meanings and other hopes—
then can be read more clearly.
Now that I sit idly and reflect,
few are the moons that remain in memory:
islands, colour of grieving Madonna, late in the waning
or moonlight in northern cities casting sometimes
over turbulent streets, rivers, and limbs of men
a heavy torpor.
Yet here last evening, in this our final port
where we wait for the hour of our return to dawn
like an old debt, money which lay for years
in a miser's safe, and at last
the time for payment came
and coins were heard falling on the table—
in this Etruscan village, behind the sea of Salerno
behind the harbours of our return, on the edge
of an autumn squall, the moon
outstripped the clouds, and houses
on the slope opposite became enamel:
Amica silentia lunae.*

This is a train of thought, a way
to begin to speak of things you confess
uneasily, at times when you can't hold back, to a friend
who fled in secret and who brings
news from home and from the companions,

and you hasten to open your heart
before this exile forestalls you and alters him.
We come from Arabia, Egypt, Palestine, Syria;
the little state
of Kommagene, which flickered out like a small lamp,
often comes to mind,
and great cities which lived for thousands of years
and then became pastures for cattle,
fields for sugar-cane and corn.
We come from the sand of the desert, from the seas of Proteus,
souls shrivelled by public sins,
each holding public office, like a bird in its cage.
The rainy autumn in this cavity
infects the wound of each of us
or what you might term differently: nemesis, fate,
or simply bad habits, fraud and deceit,
or even the selfish urge to reap reward from the blood of others.
Man frays easily in wars;
man is soft, a sheaf of grass,
lips and fingers that hunger for a white breast
eyes that half-close in the radiance of day
and feet that would run, no matter how tired,
at the slightest call of profit.
Man is soft and thirsty like grass,
insatiable like grass, his nerves roots that stretch out;
when the harvest comes
he would rather have the scythes whistle in some other field;
when the harvest comes
some call out to exorcise the demon
some become entangled in their riches, others make orations.
But what good are exorcisms, riches, orations
when the living are far away?
Is man any different?
Is it not this which confers life:
a time for planting, a time for harvesting?

GEORGE SEFERIS

The same things over and over again, you will say, my friend,
But the thought of the refugee, the thought of the prisoner, the
      thought
of man when he too has become a commodity—
try though you may, you cannot change it.
He might even have wished to remain king of the cannibals
expending powers which no one buys,
to promenade in fields of agapanthi
to hear the drums beneath a bamboo tree,
as courtiers dance with prodigious masks.
But the country which they chop up and burn like a pine-tree,
      and which you see
either in the dark train, without water, the windows broken,
      night after night
or in the burning ship which, as the statistics indicate, will surely
      sink,
these things have taken root in the mind and do not change
these things have planted images like those trees
which in virgin forests cast their branches
and these take root in the earth and sprout again;
they cast their branches which sprout again, striding league
      after league—
and our mind a virgin forest of slain friends.
And if I speak to you in fables and parables
it is because you hear it more gently, and horror
cannot be talked about because it is alive
because it is speechless and continuous:
the memory-wounding pain
drips by day drips in sleep.*

To speak of heroes to speak of heroes: Michael
who fled from the hospital with open wounds
perhaps he spoke of heroes—the night
he dragged his foot through the darkened city—
when, groping, he howled out our pain: "We advance in the dark,

we go forward in the dark . . ."
The heroes go forward in the dark.

Few the moonlit nights that have pleased me.

"Thrush" *

Δαίμονος ἐπιπόνου καὶ τύχης χαλεπῆς
ἐφήμερον σπέρμα, τί με βιάζεσθε
λέγειν, ἃ ὑμῖν ἄρειον μὴ γνῶναι.

Silenus to Midas

I
The House Near the Sea

The houses that I had were taken from me. It happened
that the years were unpropitious: wars, ruins, exiles;
sometimes the hunter finds the migratory birds,
sometimes he does not find them. Hunting
was good in my time, many felt the pellet;
the rest circle aimlessly or go mad in the shelters.

Do not speak to me of the nightingale nor of the lark
nor of the little wagtail
inscribing figures with his tail in the light;
I do not know much about houses
I know they have their own nature, nothing else.
New at first, like babies
who play in gardens with the tassels of the sun,
they embroider coloured shutters and shining doors
upon the day.
When the architect has finished, they change,
they frown or smile or even grow stubborn
with those who remained, with those who went away
with others who would return if they but could
or others who vanished, now that the world has become
a limitless hotel.

I do not know much about houses,

I remember their joy and their sorrow
sometimes, when I pause;
                and again
sometimes, near the sea, in naked rooms
with a single iron bed and nothing of my own
watching the evening spider, I reflect
that someone is getting ready to come, that they adorn him *
with white and black robes, with many-coloured jewels,
and around him is the quiet talk of venerable ladies—
grey hair and dark lace shawls—
that he is getting ready to come and say goodbye to me
or that a woman—eyelashes curled, deep-girdled,
returning from southern harbours,
Smyrna Rhodes Syracuse Alexandria,
from cities closed like hot shutters,
with perfume of golden fruit and herbs—
climbs the stairs without noticing
those who sleep beneath the stairs.

You know, houses grow stubborn easily when you strip them
        bare.

II
Sensual Elpenor

I saw him yesterday standing by the door
below my window; it was about
seven o'clock; a woman was with him.
He had the look of Elpenor just before he fell
and smashed himself, and yet he was not drunk.
He was speaking rapidly, and she
was gazing absentmindedly towards the gramophones;
now and then she cut him short to say a word
and then would glance impatiently

128

there where they were frying fish: like a cat.
He whispered with a dead cigarette butt in his lips:

—"Listen also to this. In the moonlight
the statues sometimes bend like reeds
among ripe fruit—the statues;
and the flame becomes a cool oleander,
the flame that burns man, I mean."

—"It is just the light . . . shadows of the night."

—"The night perhaps which opened, a blue pomegranate,
a dark breast, and filled you with stars,
arresting time.
                              And yet the statues
bend sometimes, dividing desire in two,
like a peach; and the flame
becomes a kiss on the limbs, a sobbing,
and then a cool leaf carried off by the wind;
they bend; they become light with a human weight.
You do not forget it."

                    —"The statues are in the museum."

—"No, they pursue you, why can't you see it?
I mean, with their broken limbs,
with a form from another time, a form you do not recognize
and yet know.
                        As when
in the last years of your youth you love
a woman who had stayed beautiful, and you fear always,
while you hold her naked at noon,
the memory that awakens in your embrace;
you fear lest the kiss still betray you
to other beds now of the past

which nonetheless could haunt you
so easily, so easily, and bring to life
images in the mirror, bodies once alive:
their sensuality.
                    As when
returning from foreign lands you chance to open
an old trunk locked up a long time
and find the tatters of clothes you used to wear
at beautiful moments, at festivals with lights
of many colours, mirrored, now becoming dim,
and there remains only the perfume of the absence
of a young form.
                         Truly, those statues are not
the fragments. You yourself are the relic;
they pursue you with a strange virginity
at home, at the office, at receptions for the celebrated,
in the unconfessed terror of sleep;
they speak of circumstances that you wish did not exist
or would exist years after your death,
and this is difficult because . . ."

                    —"The statues are in the museum.
Good night."

                    —". . . because the statues are no longer
fragments. We are. The statues bend lightly . . . Good night."

Here they separated. He went
uphill towards the north
and she moved on towards the light-flooded beach
where the wave is drowned in the radio's din:

                         The Radio

          "Sails puffed out by the wind
          alone remain in the mind.

130

Perfume of silence and pine
will soon be an anodyne
now that the sailor set sail,
flycatcher, catfish, and wagtail.
O woman whose touch is dumb,
hear the wind's requiem.

"Drained is the golden keg
the sun has become a rag
round a middle-aged woman's neck—
who coughs and coughs without break;
for the summer that's gone she sighs,
for the gold on her shoulders, her thighs.
O woman, O sightless thing,
hear the blindman sing.

"Close the shutters: daylight recedes;
make flutes from yesteryear's reeds
and don't open, knock how they may:
they shout, but they've nothing to say.
Take cyclamen, pine-needles, the lily,
anemones out of the sea
O woman whose wits are lost,
hear the water's ghost.

"Athens. The public has heard
the news with alarm; it is feared
a crisis is near. The prime
minister spoke: 'There is no more time . . .'
Take cyclamen . . . needles of pine . . .
the lily . . . needles of pine . . .
O woman . . .
   —. . . is crushingly stronger
The war . . ."
  SOULMONGER *

III
The Wreck "Thrush"

"This wood which cooled my forehead
at times when the noon burned my veins
will flower in other hands. Take it, I give it to you;
look, it is wood from a lemon tree . . ."
                          I heard the voice
as I was looking at the sea trying to distinguish
a ship which they had sunk there years ago;
they called it "Thrush"—a small wreck; the masts,
broken, swayed at odd angles in the depths, like tentacles,
or the memory of dreams, marking the hull:
vague mouth of some huge dead sea-monster
extinguished in the water. Calm spread all around.

And other voices slowly followed *
in their turn; whispers thin and thirsty
emerging from the other side of the sun, the dark side;
one would say they longed to drink a drop of blood;
familiar voices, but I could not make them out.
And the voice of the old man came; this one I felt
falling to the heart of day,
still, as though motionless:
"And if you condemn me to drink poison, I thank you.
Your law shall be my law; how can I go
wandering about in foreign lands, a rolling stone.
I prefer death.
Only God knows which of us will prosper."

Lands of the sun and you cannot face the sun.
Lands of man and you cannot face man.

GEORGE SEFERIS

The Light

As the years pass
the judges who condemn you multiply;
as the years pass and you talk with fewer voices,
you see the sun with other eyes:
you know that those who remained were deceiving
        you
the delirium of flesh, the lovely dance
that ends in nakedness.
As when, turning at night in the empty highway,
you suddenly see the eyes of an animal shine,
eyes already gone: so you sense your own eyes:
you gaze at the sun, then you are lost in the dark.
The doric chiton
that swayed like the mountains when your fingers
        touched it
is a marble figure in the light, but its head is in the
        dark.
And those who left the palestra with their bows
struck the willing marathon runner
and he saw the track sail in blood,
the world empty like the moon,
the gardens of victory wither:
you see them in the sun, behind the sun.
And the boys who dive from the bow-sprits
go like spindles twisting still,
naked bodies plunging into black light
with a coin between the teeth, swimming still,
while the sun with golden needles sews
sails and wet wood and colours of the sea;
and still down they go
slanting
towards stones of the deep—
white lekythoi.

Light angelic and black,
laughter of waves on the sea's highway,
tear-stained laughter,
the aged suppliant sees you
as he moves to cross the invisible fields— *
light mirrored in his blood,
the blood which gave birth to Eteocles and Poly-
          nices.
Day angelic and black;
the brackish taste of woman that poisons the
          prisoner
emerges from the wave a cool branch adorned
          with drops.
Sing little Antigone, sing, O sing . . .
I do not speak to you of things past, I speak of love;
trim your hair with the sun's thorns,
dark girl.
The heart of the Scorpion has set,*
the tyrant within man has fled,
and all the daughters of the sea, Nereids, Graeae,*
hurry to the radiance of the rising goddess:
whoever has never loved shall love,
in the light:
                    and you find yourself
in a large house with many windows open
running from room to room, not knowing from
          where to look out first,
because the pine-trees will vanish, and the mir-
          rored mountains, and the chirping of
          birds
the sea will drain dry, shattered glass, from north
          and south
your eyes will empty of the light of day—
how suddenly and all together the cicadas cease.

GEORGE SEFERIS

Agianapa I *

And you see the light of the sun as the ancients used to say.
And yet I thought I had been seeing all these years
walking between the mountains and the sea
meeting by chance men in perfect armour;
strange, I did not notice that I saw their voices only.
It was blood that made them talk, the ram
that I slew and then spread at their feet;
but that red carpet was not the light.
Whatever they told me I had to recognize by touch
as when they hide you at night, hunted, in a stable
or when you finally reach the body of a deep breasted woman
and the room is full of suffocating odours;
whatever they told me, skin and silk.

Strange, here I see the light of the sun; the golden net
where things quiver like fish
that a huge angel draws in
along with the nets of the fisherman.

Engomi *

Broad the plain and level; visible from a distance
the turning of arms that dug.
In the sky, the clouds all curves, here and there
a trumpet golden and rose: the sunset.
In the sparse grass and the thorns
stirred light after-shower air: it had rained
there on the peaks where the mountains took on colour.

And I moved on towards those at work,
women and men digging with picks in trenches.
It was an ancient city; walls, roads and houses
stood out like the petrified muscles of cyclopes,
the anatomy of spent strength under the eye
of the archaeologist, anaesthetist, or surgeon.
Phantasms and fabrics, luxury and lips, buried
and the curtains of pain spread wide open
to reveal, naked and indifferent, the tomb.

And I looked towards those at work,
the stretched shoulders and the arms that struck
this dead silence with a rhythm heavy and swift
as though the wheel of fate were passing through the ruins.

Suddenly I was walking and did not walk
I looked at the flying birds, and they were turned to marble
I looked at the sky's air, and it was full of wonder
I looked at the bodies that struggled, and they had stopped
and among them the light bringing forth a face.
The black hair spilled over the collar, the eyebrows
had the flutter of swallows, the nostrils
arched above the lips, and the body

emerged from the labouring hands stripped
with the unripe breasts of the Virgin,
a dance motionless.

And I lowered my eyes all round:
girls kneaded, but they did not touch the dough
women spun, but the spindles did not turn
lambs were being watered, but their tongues hung still
above green waters that seemed asleep
and the shepherd remained with his crook poised.*
and I looked again at that body ascending;
many had gathered, ants,
and they struck her with lances but did not wound her.
Her belly now shone like the moon
and I thought the sky was the womb
which bore her and took her back, mother and child.
Her feet remained marble still
and vanished: an Assumption.
                                            The world
became again as it had been, ours
with time and earth.
                            Aromas of mastic
began to stir on the old slopes of memory
breasts among leaves, lips moist;
and all went dry at once on the length of the plain,
in the stone's despair, in the corroded power,
in that empty place with the sparse grass and the thorns
where a snake slithered heedless
where it takes a long time to die.

Δ. Ι. Ἀντωνίου

IV D. I. ANTONIOU

Obstacle to What

Obstacle to what?

I recalled the signal's greeting
as you sighted us from four miles away
when we returned after many years.

You recognized the ship
with the blond hero's name
—seed of the sea with a landsman's fate—.

We brought you no more than stories
of distant places, memories
of precious things, of perfumes.

Do not seek their weight upon your hands;
your hands should be less human
for all we held in exile;
the experience of touch, the struggle of
       weight,
exotic colours
you should feel in our words only
this night of our return.

Obstacle to what
the mast that told you
of our return?

Tonight You Remembered

Tonight you remembered the beginning
the evening of rain when you decided
to make experience of the nostalgia for
        distant places
that left us useless
for life.

We asked you to pity us Lord,
seed of a gaudy flowering
in the barren earth.
Crushed to the point of silent prayer
ruined to the point of desperation,
we longed for the fate of simple men,
the astonishment of the ignorant.
Empty us if you would of all we know
give us—we cried within ourselves—
fatigue
after an honest struggle.

Condescension!
the decision: to take the road we took
until the end; from where we fell
to rise again.
Do not give us practical dreams,
do not awaken the magnets of inherit-
        ance:
prows that lose themselves and find
        themselves out at sea.
In our anonymous struggles deliver us;
from where we fell to rise
winning the victory
body to body.

D. I. ANTONIOU

Should We Turn Back

Should we turn back?
—sorrow waits for us in the past:
what you failed to exhaust on journeys,
baring your heart—
Yet for one return
you rave,
moments when you gave away all
for an unrepenting wisdom!

You remember when reading the Florentine for the
       first time
as a boy—how near those years are tonight—
you said look! that cross there, embroidered with stars.
Their flowers would make me drunk, you said,
reading ancient Indian books.

The climate that makes you live in the nostalgia
of a landscape beneath the southern sky—
the colours are missing for you to picture it,
the caress is missing from the language you speak.
So the whole of you,
in the language you chose to wear,
longs to tell of the colour of an agate's gentle glow
in the meadow spread there deep in memory.

Calm down. Succeed in declaring yourself.

A Hunted Moon Was Caught

A hunted moon was caught
in the naked and desolate branches of winter.
Don't you remember the sunset,
the purple that flamed in the black of your hair;
your realm, the night, lying down in its dreams,
ruled the same moon . . .
You don't remember . . .
nor does it remember now
it forgets,
recalling only journeys and drownings in the night
dream-bewitched and nightmarish
dawning days which brought it to a bed of near
       death,
caught up in the storm
hunted, the clouds calling it
and you rejoiced in its confusion
all that I don't forget remembers you now
hunted shepherdess
without words, salvation of your solitude;
words of poets, a heavy shield
in the battle of a dream's bitter immortality . . .

’Οδυσσέας ’Ελύτης

V   ODYSSEUS ELYTIS

The Mad Pomegranate Tree

Inquisitive matinal high spirits *à perdre haleine*

In these all-white courtyards where the south wind blows
Whistling through vaulted arcades, tell me, is it the mad pome-
    granate tree
That leaps in the light, scattering its fruitful laughter
With windy wilfulness and whispering, tell me, is it the mad
    pomegranate tree
That quivers with foliage newly born at dawn
Raising high its colours in a shiver of triumph?

On plains where the naked girls awake,
When they harvest clover with their light brown arms
Roaming round the borders of their dreams—tell me, is it the
    mad pomegranate tree,
Unsuspecting, that puts the lights in their verdant baskets
That floods their names with the singing of birds—tell me
Is it the mad pomegranate tree that combats the cloudy skies of
    the world?

On the day that it adorns itself in jealousy with seven kinds of
    feathers,
Girding the eternal sun with a thousand blinding prisms
Tell me, is it the mad pomegranate tree
That seizes on the run a horse's mane of a hundred lashes,
Never sad and never grumbling—tell me, is it the mad pome-
    granate tree
That cries out the new hope now dawning?

Tell me, is that the mad pomegranate tree waving in the dis-
    tance,

Fluttering a handkerchief of leaves of cool flame,
A sea near birth with a thousand ships and more,
With waves that a thousand times and more set out and go
To unscented shores—tell me, is it the mad pomegranate tree
That creaks the rigging aloft in the lucid air?

High as can be, with the blue bunch of grapes that flares and
     celebrates
Arrogant, full of danger—tell me, is it the mad pomegranate tree
That shatters with light the demon's tempests in the middle of
     the world
That spreads far as can be the saffron ruffle of day
Richly embroidered with scattered songs—tell me, is it the mad
     pomegranate tree
That unfastens with haste the silk apparel of day?

In petticoats of April first and cicadas of the feast of mid-August
Tell me, that which plays, that which rages, that which can
     entice
Shaking out of threats their evil black darkness
Spilling in the sun's embrace intoxicating birds
Tell me, that which opens its wings on the breast of things
On the breast of our deepest dreams, is that the mad pome-
     granate tree?

ODYSSEUS ELYTIS

Marina of the Rocks

You have a taste of tempest on your lips—But where did you
　　　wander
All day long in the hard reverie of stone and sea?
An eagle-bearing wind stripped the hills
Stripped your longing to the bone
And the pupils of your eyes received the message of chimera
Spotting memory with foam!
Where is the familiar slope of short September
On the red earth where you played, looking down
At the broad rows of the other girls
The corners where your friends left armfuls of rosemary.

But where did you wander
All night long in the hard reverie of stone and sea?
I told you to count in the naked water its luminous days
On your back to rejoice in the dawn of things
Or again to wander on yellow plains
With a clover of light on your breast, heroine of iambs.

You have a taste of tempest on your lips
And a dress red as blood
Deep in the gold of summer
And the perfume of hyacinths—But where did you wander
Descending toward the shores, the pebbled bays?
There was cold salty seaweed there
But deeper a human feeling that bled
And you opened your arms in astonishment naming it
Climbing lightly to the clearness of the depths
Where your own star-fish shone.

Listen. The word is the prudence of the aged
And time is a passionate sculptor of men

And the sun stands over it, a beast of hope
And you, closer to it, embrace a love
With a bitter taste of tempest on your lips.

It is not for you, blue to the bone, to think of another sum-
        mer,
For the rivers to change their bed
And take you back to their mother
For you to kiss other cherry trees
Or ride on the north-west wind.

Propped on the rocks, without yesterday or tomorrow,
Facing the dangers of the rocks with a hurricane's hairdo
You will say farewell to the riddle that is yours.

ODYSSEUS ELYTIS

Commemoration

I brought my life this far
To this spot which struggles
Forever near the sea
Youth upon the rocks, breast
To breast against the wind
Where is a man to go
Who is nothing other than a man
Reckoning with the coolness his green
Moments, with waters the visions
Of his hearing, with wings his remorse
O Life
Of a child who becomes a man
Forever near the sea when the sun
Teaches him to breathe there where the
         shadow
Of a seagull vanishes.

I brought my life this far
White addition, black total
A few trees and a few
Wet pebbles
Gentle fingers to caress a forehead
What forehead
Anticipation wept all night and is no more
Nor is anyone.
Were but a free footstep to be heard
A rested voice to rise
The poops to ripple at the jetty, inscribing
A name in darker blue upon their horizon
A few years, a few waves
Sensitive rowing
In the bays surrounding love

I brought my life this far
Bitter furrow in the sand which will vanish
—Whoever saw two eyes touch his silence
And mixed with their sunshine, closing a
       thousand worlds
Let him remind his blood in other suns
Nearer the light

There is a smile that pays for the flame—
But here in this ignorant landscape that
       loses itself
In an open and merciless sea
Success sheds
Whirling feathers
And moments that have become attached to
       the earth
Hard earth under the soles of impatient feet
Earth made for vertigo
A dead volcano.

I brought my life this far
A stone pledged to the liquid element
Beyond the islands
Lower than the waves
Next to the anchors
—When keels pass, splitting with passion
Some new obstacle, and triumph over it
And hope dawns with all its dolphins
The sun's gain in a human heart—
The nets of doubt draw in
A figure in salt
Carved with effort
Indifferent, white,
Which turns toward the sea the void of its
       eyes
Supporting infinity.

Body of Summer

A long time has passed since the last rain was heard
Above the ants and lizards
Now the sun burns endlessly
The fruit paints its mouth
The pores in the earth open slowly
And beside the water that drips in syllables
A huge plant gazes into the eye of the sun.

Who is he that lies on the shores beyond
Stretched on his back, smoking silver-burnt olive
       leaves?
Cicadas grow warm in his ears
Ants are at work on his chest
Lizards slide in the grass of his arm pits
And over the seaweed of his feet a wave rolls lightly
Sent by the little siren that sang:

"O body of summer, naked, burnt
Eaten away by oil and salt
Body of rock and shudder of the heart
Great ruffling wind in the osier hair
Breath of basil above the curly pubic mound
Full of stars and pine needles
Body, deep vessel of the day!

"Soft rains come, violent hail
The land passes lashed into the claws of the north
      wind
Which darkens in the depths with furious waves
The hills plunge into the dense udders of the clouds

And yet behind all this you laugh carefree
And find your deathless moment again
As the sun finds you again on the sandy shores
As the sky finds you again in your naked health."

Drinking the Sun of Corinth

Drinking the sun of Corinth
Reading the marble ruins
Striding across vineyards and seas
Sighting along the harpoon
A votive fish that slips away
I found the leaves that the psalm of the sun
       memorizes
The living land that desire opens joyously.

I drink water, cut fruit,
Thrust my hand into the wind's foliage
The lemon trees irrigate the pollen of sum-
       mer
The green birds tear my dreams
I leave with a glance
A wide glance in which the world is recre-
       ated
Beautiful from the beginning to the dimen-
       sions of the heart!

This Wind that Loiters

This wind that loiters among the quinces
This bug that sucks the vines
This stone that the scorpion wears next to his skin
And these stacks on the threshing floor
That play the giant to small barefoot children.

The images of the Resurrection
On walls that the pine-trees scratched with their fingers
This whitewash that carries the noonday on its back
And the cicadas, the cicadas in the ears of the trees.

Great summer of chalk
Great summer of cork
The red sails slanting in gusts of wind
On the sea-floor white creatures, sponges
Accordions of the rocks
Perch from the fingers even of bad fishermen
Proud reefs on the fishing lines of the sun.

No one will tell our fate, and that is that.
We ourselves will tell the sun's fate, and that is that.

All Day Long We Walked in the Fields

All day long we walked in the fields
With our women, suns, and dogs
We played, sang, drank water
Fresh as it sprang from the ages

In the afternoon we sat for a moment
And we looked deeply into each other's eyes
A butterfly flew from our hearts
It was whiter
Than the small white branch at the tip of
       our dreams
We knew that it was never to disappear
That it did not remember at all what worms
       it bore

At night we lit a fire
And round about it sang:

Fire, lovely fire, do not pity the logs
Fire, lovely fire, do not turn to ash
Fire, lovely fire, burn us
         tell us of life.

We tell of life, we take it by the hands
We look into its eyes and it returns our look
And if this which makes us drunk is a mag-
      net, we know it
And if this which gives us pain is bad, we
      have felt it

We tell of life, we go ahead
And say farewell to its birds, which are mi-
      grating

We are of a good generation.

With What Stones, What Blood,
and What Iron

With what stones, what blood, and what iron,
With what fire are we made
Though we seem pure mist
And they stone us and say
That we walk with our heads in the clouds
How we pass our days and nights
God only knows

My friend, when night wakens your electric grief
I see the tree of the heart spreading
Your arms open beneath a pure Idea
To which you call
But which will not descend
For years and years:
It up there, and you down here

And yet longing's vision awakens flesh one day
And there where only bare solitude once shone
A city now laughs lovely as you would have it
You almost see it, it is waiting for you
Give me your hand so that we may go there be-
        fore the Dawn
Floods it with cries of triumph

Give me your hand—before birds gather
On the shoulders of men to announce in song
That Virginal Hope is seen coming at last
Out of the distant sea.

We will go together, and let them stone us
And let them say we walk with our heads in the
      clouds—
Those who have never felt, my friend,
With what iron, what stones, what blood, what
      fire,
We build, dream, and sing.

I Lived the Beloved Name

I lived the beloved name
In the shade of the aged olive tree
In the roaring of the lifelong sea

Those who stoned me live no longer
With their stones I built a fountain
To its brink green girls come
Their lips descend from the dawn
Their hair unwinds far into the future

Swallows come, infants of the wind
They drink, they fly, so that life goes on
The threat of the dream becomes a dream
Pain rounds the good cape
No voice is lost in the breast of the sky

O deathless sea, tell me what you are whis-
      pering
I reach your morning mouth early
On the peak where your love appears
I see the will of the night spilling stars
The will of the day nipping the earth's shoots

I saw a thousand wild lilies on the meadows
      of life
A thousand children in the true wind
Beautiful strong children who breathe out
      kindness
And know how to gaze at the deep horizons
When music raises the islands

I carved the beloved name
In the shade of the aged olive tree
In the roaring of the lifelong sea.

The Autopsy

And so, they found that the gold of the olive-root had dripped in
the recesses of his heart.

And from the many times that he had lain awake by candlelight
waiting for the dawn, a strange heat had seized his en-
trails.

A little below the skin, the blue line of the horizon sharply
painted. And ample traces of blue throughout his blood.

The cries of birds which he had come to memorize in hours of
great loneliness apparently spilled out all at once, so that
it was impossible for the knife to enter deeply.

Probably the intention sufficed for the evil

Which he met—it is obvious—in the terrifying posture of the
innocent. His eyes open, proud, the whole forest moving
still on the unblemished retina.

Nothing in the brain but a dead echo of the sky.

Only in the hollow of his left ear some light fine sand, as though
in a shell. Which means that often he had walked by the
sea alone, with the pain of love and the roar of the wind.

As for those particles of fire on his thighs, they show that he
moved time hours ahead whenever he embraced a
woman.

We shall have early fruit this year.

Beauty and the Illiterate

Often, at the Dormition of Twilight, her soul took on a certain *
lightness from the mountains opposite, though the day
had been cruel and tomorrow was unknown.

Yet, when darkness came and the hand of the priest appeared
over the garden of the dead, She,

Alone, Erect, with the few familiar companions of night—the
rosemary breeze and the charcoal smoke from chimneys
—lay awake on the threshold of the sea

Singularly beautiful.

Words half-formed of waves or half-guessed in a rustling, and
others seemingly of the dead, words startled among the
cypresses, like strange Zodiacs circling her head, suddenly illumined her. And an

Unbelievable clarity allowed the true landscape to appear at a
great depth within her,

Where, beside the river, black men fought the Angel, showing in
what manner Beauty is born

Or what in other terms we call tears.

And as long as her thought lasted, you felt that it overflowed her
shining face, with the bitterness in the eyes and the
cheekbones—like those of an ancient temple-servant—
enormous

Stretching from the tip of Canis Major to the tip of Virgo.

"And I, far from the pestilence of the city, imagined a desert at
    her side, where tears would have no meaning and where
    the only light would be that of the fire which devoured all
    my possessions

The two of us shoulder to shoulder would sustain the weight of
    the future, sworn to utter silence and to a condominion of
    the stars

As though I did not know, illiterate as I am, that it is exactly
    there, in utter silence, where the most appalling noises
    are heard

And that loneliness, from the time it became unendurable to the
    heart of man, has scattered and sown stars!"

Νίκος Γκάτσος

VI   NIKOS GATSOS

In the Griever's Courtyard

In the griever's courtyard no sun rises
Only worms appear to mock the stars
Only horses sprout upon the ant hills
And bats eat birds and cast off sperm.

In the griever's courtyard night never sets
Only the foliage vomits forth a river of tears
When the devil passes by to mount the dogs
And the crows swim in a well of blood.

In the griever's courtyard the eye has gone dry
The brain has frozen and the heart turned to stone
Frog-flesh hangs from the spider's teeth
Hungry locusts scream at the vampire's feet.

In the griever's courtyard black grass grows
Only one night in May did a breeze pass by
A step light as a tremor on the meadow
A kiss of the foam-trimmed sea.

And should you thirst for water, we will wring a cloud
And should you hunger for bread, we will kill a night-
        ingale
Only wait a moment for the wild rue to open,
For the black sky to flash, the mullen to flower.

But it was a breeze that vanished, a lark that disap-
        peared
It was the face of May, the moon's whiteness
A step light as a tremor on the meadow
A kiss of the foam-trimmed sea.

They Say the Mountains Tremble

They say the mountains tremble and the fir-trees rage
When night gnaws the tile-pins to let in the kallikant-
      zari *
When hell gulps down the torrents' foaming toil
Or when the hair of the pepper-tree becomes the north-
      wind's plaything.

Only Achaean cattle graze vigorous and strong
On abundant fields in Thessaly beneath an ageless,
      watching sun
They eat green grass and celery, leaves of the poplar
      tree, they drink clear water in the troughs
They smell the sweat of the earth and then fall heavily
      to sleep in the shade of the willow tree.

"Cast out the dead" said Heraclitus and saw the sky turn
      pale
And saw two small cyclamens kissing in the mud
And as the wolf comes down from the woods to see the
      dog's carcass and to weep,
He too fell to kiss his own dead body in the hospitable soil.
What good to me the bead that glistens on your forehead?
I know the lightning wrote its name upon your lips
I know an eagle built its nest within your eyes
But here on this damp bank there is one way only
One deceptive way and you must take it
You must plunge into blood before time forestalls you,
Cross over opposite to find your companions again
Flowers birds deer
To find another sea, another tenderness,
To take Achilles' horses by the reins

Instead of sitting dumb scolding the river
Stoning the river like the mother of Kitso *
Because you too will be lost and your beauty will have aged.
I see your childhood shirt drying on the branches of a wil-
      low
Take it, this flag of life, to shroud your death
And may your heart not fail you
And may your tear not fall upon this pitiless earth
As a penguin's tear once fell in the frozen wilderness
Complaint achieves nothing
Everywhere life will be the same
With the serpent's flute in the land of phantoms
With the song of brigands in aromatic groves
With the knife of some sorrow in the cheek of hope
With the pain of some spring in a wood-owl's heart;
Enough to find a sharp sickle and a plough in a joyful hand
Enough if a little wheat flowers for the feasts
A little wine for remembrance, a little water for the dust.

Death and the Knight

(1513) *

As I behold you motionless
journeying through the ages with the steed of Akritas and
       the lance of Saint George,*
I could place near you,
with these dark forms that will assist you always,
until one day you too will vanish with them forever,
until you become a fire again in the great womb of Fate
       that gave you birth,
I could place near you
a bitter orange-tree in the snow-covered meadows of the
       moon,
could unfold before you the veil of some evening,
with the red star of Scorpio singing of youth
with the River of Heaven spilling into August
with the North Star weeping and freezing,
I could place pastures,
streams that once watered the lilies of Germany,
and this armour that you wear, I could adorn it
with a basil-shoot and a spray of mint
with the weapons of Plapoutas and Nikitaras' trophies.*
But I who saw your descendants like birds
tear the sky of my country one spring dawn,
saw the cypresses of Morea hush
there on the plain of Nauplia,
before the ready embrace of the wounded sea,
where the centuries have fought with the crosses of cour-
       age,
I will now place near you
the embittered eyes of a child,

the closed eyelids
in the mud and blood of Holland.

This black land
will grow green some day
The iron hand of Goetz will overturn the carts,*
will load them with sheaves of barley and rye,
and in the dark forests with their dead loves,
there where time turned a virgin leaf to stone,
on breasts where a tearful rose trembled lightly,
a silent star will shine like a spring daisy.

But you will stay motionless;
with the steed of Akritas and the lance of St. George
you will journey through the ages,
a restless hunter of the generation of heroes,
with these dark forms that will assist you always,
until one day you too will vanish with them forever,
until you become a fire again in the great womb of Fate
          that gave you birth,
until again in the river caves resound
heavy hammers of patience
not for rings and swords *
but for pruning-knives and ploughs.

NOTES

The Greek texts of the poems offered here can be found in the following sources:

C. P. Cavafis, *Poems*, Alexandrinês Technês, Alexandria, 1935.

Κ. Π. Καβάφης, Ποιήματα, Ἀλεξανδρινῆς Τέχνης, Ἀλεξάνδρια, 1935.

C. P. Cavafis, *Poems*, Ikaros, Athens, 1948.

Κ. Π. Καβάφης, Ποιήματα, Ἴκαρος, Ἀθήνα, 1948.

Anghelos Sikelianos, *Lyrical Life*, 3 vols., Philoi Tou Bibliou, Athens, 1946–1947.

Ἄγγελος Σικελιανός, Λυρικός Βίος, 3 τόμοι, Φίλοι τοῦ Βιβλίου, Ἀθήνα, 1946–1947.

George Seferis, *Poems: 1924–1946*, Ikaros, Athens, 1950.

Γιῶργος Σεφέρης, Ποιήματα: 1924–1946, Ἴκαρος, Ἀθήνα, 1950.

George Seferis, . . . Κύπρον, οὗ μ᾽ἐθέσπισεν . . . , Ikaros, Athens, 1955.

Γιῶργος Σεφέρης, . . . Κύπρον, οὗ μ᾽ἐθέσπισεν . . . , Ἴκαρος, Ἀθήνα, 1955.

D. I. Antoniou, *Poems*, Athens, 1939; and in *Angloellinikê Epitheorisê*, Vol. 7, No. 5, Athens, 1954.

Δ. Ι. Ἀντωνίου, Ποιήματα, Ἀθήνα, 1939, καί στήν Ἀγγλοελληνική Ἐπιθεώρηση, τομ. 7, ἀρ. 5, Ἀθήνα, 1954.

Odysseus Elytis, *Orientations*, Pyrsos, Athens, 1940.

Ὀδυσσέας Ἐλύτης, Προσανατολισμοί, Πυρσός, Ἀθήνα, 1940.

Odysseus Elytis, *The First Sun*, O Glaros, Athens, 1943.

Ὀδυσσέας Ἐλύτης, Ἥλιος ὁ Πρῶτος, Ὁ Γλάρος, Ἀθήνα, 1943.

Odysseus Elytis, *Six and One Regrets for the Sky*, Ikaros, 1960.

Ὀδυσσέας Ἐλύτης, Ἔξη καί μία τύψεις γιά τόν Οὐρανό, Ἴκαρος, Ἀθήνα, 1960.

Nikos Gatsos, *Amorgos*, Aetos, Athens, 1943; and in E. N. Apostolides, *Anthology: 1708–1952*, "Estias," Athens, 1954.

Νίκος Γκάτσος, Ἀμοργός, Ἀετός, Ἀθήνα, 1943, καί στοῦ Η. Ν. Ἀποστολίδη τήν Ἀνθολογία:1708–1952, Βιβλιοπωλεῖον τῆς "Ἑστίας," Ἀθήνα, 1954.

NOTES

We have kept the following notes as short as possible, including only that material which we consider may be of use to the English-speaking reader. Fuller studies of the work of some of the poets included in this anthology as well as of modern Greek poetry in general may be found in *The Marble Threshing Floor*, Studies in Modern Greek Poetry, by Philip Sherrard (London, 1955); and in "George Seferis and Stratis the Mariner," *Accent*, Summer, 1956, and "T. S. Eliot and the Poetry of George Seferis," *Comparative Literature*, Summer, 1956, both by Edmund Keeley. Fuller notes to the poetry of Cavafy are contained in John Mavrogordato's volume of translations, *The Poems of C. P. Cavafy, loc. cit.*, and to Seferis's poetry in the two volumes of his work cited opposite.

Page

34   The title. Cf. Plutarch, *Life of Antony,* par. 75, and Shakespeare, *Antony and Cleopatra,* IV, iii.

38   The title. "To what extent Hellenism had penetrated the Parthian court at the time we do not know, but it is obvious that the Arsacids were fain to present themselves to their Greek subjects as sympathetic protectors. The money of the kingdom was stamped exclusively with Greek legends, and from the time of Mithridates I, they commonly added to their other surnames that of 'Philhellene.' But they were unable to make the Greeks overlook the difference between a barbarian and a western dynasty." Edwyn Bevan, *The House of Seleucus* (London, 1902), Vol. II, p. 159.

39   Line 12. Plutarch, in his *Life of Pompey*, says that Theodotus of Chios persuaded the Egyptians to kill Pompey when he landed.

40   The title. Manuel Comnenos was Byzantine Emperor, 1143–1180.

42   Line 16. In the spring of A.D. 68, C. Julius Vindex, governor of Lugdunensis, rose against Nero; Galba (later Emperor Servius Sulpicius Galba) was invited to replace Nero, and he made his troops in Spain proclaim him a legate of the Senate and of the Roman people. The Praetorians, bribed to acclaim Galba, de-

serted Nero, who fled from Rome, and, on 9 June 68, committed suicide. Galba took the title of Caesar and went to Rome.

44   The title. Demetrius Soter was one of the grandchildren of Antiochus the Great, the King of Syria, who had lost his kingdom to the Romans at the Battle of Magnesia in 190 B.C. Demetrius Soter was sent to Rome as a hostage, but on the death of Antiochus he asked to be set free. The Senate refused, and so he escaped secretly. He returned to Syria, the people declared in his favour, and finally he obtained recognition as king from the Romans. He expelled the satrap Heracleides from Babylon, thus earning the title Soter. But through the excesses of his life he lost his people's support, was overthrown by an imposter, Balas, and killed by him in battle.

46   Line 6. Mithridates VI, Eupator Dionysus (the "Great") was the last of a line of kings of the Pontus of the same name.

48   Line 10. Botaneiatis is the Byzantine Emperor Nikephoros III Botaneiatis, dethroned in 1081 by Alexios I Comnenos, whose wife was the Irene Doukaina mentioned here.

50   Line 1. The philosopher Ammonius (d. A.D. 243; "Sakkas" because he had been a sack-carrier) taught at Alexandria and is supposed to have had both Plotinus and Origen among his pupils.

52   The title. The quotation heading this poem is from a satirical work of the Emperor Julian the Apostate in which he upbraids the people of Antioch, then a Christian city, for their hostile attitude towards his attempts to restore his prudish and moralistic form of paganism. The poem is the response of the Antiochians to Julian's pedantic reproof.

53   Line 25. In 363 the Emperor Julian was killed and Jovian, a Christian, was elected in his stead. Jovian's support of orthodoxy made him, for the Christians, a welcome successor to Julian (in Syrian literature he even became the subject of a Christian romance), and the poem expresses the relief of the Antiochians at the change. See also *Julian and the Antiochians*.

56   The title. Kleomenes (King of Sparta 236–222 B.C.) had agreed to send his mother, Kratesiclea, and his children as hostages to Egypt on the condition that Ptolemy III Euergetes, King of Egypt, would send him aid in his war against Macedonia and

the Achaean League. (See Plutarch's *Life of Agis and Kleo-menes*.)

61 Line 2. Zabinas, Grypos, and Hyrcanus are in fact historical personages, but from the point of view of the poem it is not important to know more about them than the text makes clear: that they had rival interests in the throne of Syria.

62 The title. See notes to *Julian and the Antiochians* and *A Great Procession of Priests and Laymen* on p. 178 (52 and 53).

78 Line 4. The honey and the pomegranate both represent the sweetness which it is hoped will fill the life of the newly-married pair.

80 The title. "After giving marriage such traits of reserve and decorum, he none the less freed men from the empty and woman-ish passion of jealous possession, by making it honourable for them, while keeping the marriage relation free from all wanton irregularities, to share with other worthy men in the begetting of children, laughing to scorn those who regard such common privileges as intolerable, and resort to murder and war rather than grant them. For example, an elderly man with a young wife, if he looked with favour and esteem on some fair and noble young man, might introduce him to her, and adopt her offspring by such a noble father as his own." Plutarch, *Life of Lycurgus*, XV, 6–7; trans. Bernadotte Perrin, *Plutarch's Lives* (London, 1928) Vol. I, pp. 251–253.

83 The title. The title of this poem, much of its imagery, and a number of allusions in it are connected with the cult of the goddess Artemis Orthia and her sanctuary on the banks of the Eurotas in Laconia, close to ancient Sparta and beneath the "bronze mountain" of Taygetus. Artemis Orthia was a huntress-goddess of the fertility of both men and beasts, and was associated with Aphrodite. The name Orthia—"upright" or "straightness"—has been variously interpreted: it may have been given to the goddess because she made those who served her stand upright; it may have had a phallic significance; or it may have referred to the upright archaic form of her idol. This idol was said to have been brought back by Orestes from the land of the Tauroi, and one of the features of the goddess's cult to which Sikelianos refers is associated with it. On being brought to Laconia the idol caused trouble, civil strife and

plague, and an oracle told the people that to end this they must wet the altar in the shrine with human blood. The victim for sacrifice was chosen by lot, and, according to Pausanias, this went on until Lykourgos substituted for it the rite of scourging young men—"and so the altar continued to be stained with gore." All young Spartans were scourged; the priestess of Orthia stood by holding the idol of the goddess, which, if the beating were not severe enough, became extremely heavy. Often the victim died under the scourging, while a prize, probably a wreath, was given to him who could endure most. Plutarch (or his authority) thought this was part of a moral training, especially suitable for future soldiers; others, e.g. Frazer, and Sikelianos in this poem, regard it as part of a ceremony of initiation and purification.

90 Line 3. Taenarum is on the coast south of Sparta. There is here the entrance to Hades from which Hercules dragged up Cerberus (see p. 91, l. 2).

92 The title. The Sacred Way is the ancient road by which the great Iakchos procession went from Athens to Eleusis for the celebration of the Eleusinian Mysteries.

101 The title. *Mythical Story* is a group of twenty-four closely related poems, with a central persona; see Introduction, pp. 13 ff. The literal meaning of the title is "novel," but it has other connotations, as the poet indicates in the following note:

> MYTHICAL STORY—it is its two components that made me choose the title of this work: MYTH, because I have used, clearly enough, a certain mythology; STORY, because I have tried to express, in a certain sequence, a state of mind as independent of me as are the characters in a novel.

The title is followed by an epigraph from Rimbaud: "Si j'ai du goût, ce n'est guères Que pour la terre et les pierres."

103 Line 4. The quotation is from Plato, *Alcibiades*, 133 B. In a note on the poem, Seferis says that these words, spoken by Socrates to Alcibiades, once gave him a sensation akin to that evoked by the following lines from Baudelaire's "La mort des amants":

> Nos deux coeurs seront deux vastes flambeaux,
> Qui réfléchiront leurs doubles lumières
> Dans nos deux esprits ces miroirs jumeaux

104 Line 13. See Homer, Od. xi. 75 ff.; in E. V. Rieu's translation, Penguin Books, 1956 (the ghost of Elpenor, Odysseus' companion, is speaking):

> . . . raise a mound for me on the shore of the great sea, in memory of an unlucky man, to mark the spot for future voyagers. Do this for me, and on my barrow plant the oar I used to pull when I was alive and on the benches with my mates.

107 Line 14. See Od. xi., and Introduction, pp. 14–15.

108 Line 13. See Euripides, *Medea*, 1–2; in Gilbert Murray's translation (the Nurse is speaking):

> Would God no Argo e'er had winged the seas
> To Colchis through the blue Symplegades

The Symplegades, through which Jason and the Argonauts had to pass, were dangerous clashing rocks at the juncture of the Bosporus and the Pontus Euxinus, or Black Sea.

109 Line 16. See Od. x. 552 ff. (trans. E. V. Rieu): "There was one called Elpenor, the youngest of the party, not much of a fighting man nor very strong in the head."

112 Line 4. See Od. xi.

112 Line 5. See Od. x. 526 (trans. E. V. Rieu): "When you have finished your invocations to the glorious fellowship of the dead, sacrifice a young lamb and a black ewe, holding their heads down towards Erebus . . ."

113 Line 1. I.e., the ruined citadel of Asine on a bluff near Nauplia; see Introduction, p. 15.

116 Line 6. See Od. xxiv. 12 ff. (trans. E. V. Rieu): ". . . past the Gates of the Sun and the region of dreams they went, and before long they reached the meadow of asphodel, which is the dwelling-place of souls, the disembodied wraiths of men."

116 Line 9. Agapanthi are African lilies; see Introduction, p. 15.

116 Line 18. See Od. x.

117 Line 19. Elpenor, to whom reference has been made in *Mythical Story* (e.g. Nos. 4 and 12), is a central figure in Seferis's myth. The poet has written of this figure as follows:

Perhaps you will ask why I write about them [Elpenor and his companions] with sympathy. Because the men who belong to this category, among the heroes (in the Homeric sense, not, for God's sake, in the Carlylian) are the most sympathetic. Even the Homeric Odysseus, when he sees Elpenor, first among the dead, pities him and sheds tears. I do not say lovable or admirable, I say sympathetic, sentimental, mediocre, wasted. . . . He [Elpenor] symbolizes those to whom we refer in daily conversation with the expression: "the poor devil." However, let us not forget that these guileless men, exactly because they are "easy," are often the best carriers of an evil which has its source elsewhere.

117   Line 22. This line is from Solomos's "The Destruction of Psara" (1825). The island of Psara was razed and its people massacred during the Greek War of Independence. The complete poem, among the more famous in modern Greece, may be rendered as follows:

> On the blackened ridge of Psara
> Glory walking alone
> Recalls the gallant young men:
> On her head she wears a crown
> Made of what little grass
> Remained on that desolate earth.

123   Line 23. See Virgil, *Aeneid*, ii, 255.

125   Lines 23–24. See Aeschylus, *Agamemnon*, 179–180.

127   The title. "Thrush" was the name of a naval transport sunk off the island of Poros during the Second World War; see section III of the poem, p. 132, lines 5–12.

128   Line 7. Elpenor (see note to p. 117, l. 19, above) appears at this point, followed by Circe; they become the protagonists of section II.

131   Line 32. The term "Soulmonger" was suggested to the poet by the *Agamemnon*, 438: "Ares, the bodymonger."

132   Line 13. See Od. xi. The voices referred to in this passage are those of the dead in Hades. "The old man" of line 18 is not Teiresias, however, but Socrates, as is indicated by lines 21–

25, which are based on the *Apology* (cf. XXVII, and Socrates' concluding statement).

134   Line 5. The "aged suppliant" mentioned here is Oedipus; the "invisible fields" are those referred to in *Oedipus at Colonus*, 1681.

134   Line 15. I.e., the star Antares of the constellation Scorpio; *cor Scorpionis*.

134   Line 17. See Hesiod, *Theogony*, 270 ff. The Nereids, daughters of Nereus and Doris, were nymphs living at the bottom of the sea, reputedly propitious to sailors—especially to the Argonauts. The Graeae, children of Phorcys and Ceto, were also reputed to be sea-nymphs: divinities of the white foam seen on waves, grey from birth and thus the incarnation of age.
The "rising goddess" of the following verse is, of course, Aphrodite.

135   The title. Agianapa (sometimes spelled Ayia Napa) is a village near the sea to the south of Famagusta, Cyprus.

136   The title. Engomi is a village to the north-west of Famagusta, Cyprus.

137   Line 9. Compare lines 21–37 of this poem to the following passage, relating to the Virgin's birth of Christ, in "The Book of James, or Protevangelium," XVIII, 2, of *The Apocryphal New Testament*, trans. Montague Rhodes James:

> Now I Joseph was walking, and I walked not. And I looked up to the air and saw the air in amazement. And I looked up unto the pole of the heaven and saw it standing still, and the fowls of the heaven without motion. And I looked upon the earth and saw a dish set, and workmen lying *by it*, and their hands were in the dish: and they that were chewing chewed not, and they that were lifting *the food* lifted it not, and they that put it to their mouth put it not thereto, but the faces of all of them were looking upward. And behold there were sheep being driven, and they went not forward but stood still; and the shepherd lifted his hand to smite them with his staff, and his hand remained up. And I looked upon the stream of the river and saw the mouths of the kids upon *the water* and they drank not. And of a sudden all things moved onward in their course.

163   Line 1. The allusion is to the Dormition of the Virgin, or the Virgin's sleep before the Assumption.

168   Line 2. "Kallikantzari" are grotesque, bestial, destructive creatures who appear at night during the twelve days between Christmas and Epiphany.

169   Line 2. "The mother of Kitso" alludes to a popular ballad from the time of the Turkish occupation of Greece. Kitso was the leader of one of the bands of Greeks fighting the Turks. He fell into the hands of the enemy, and as he was about to be hanged, his mother tried to join him but found her way stopped by a river. In the ballad she is pictured as rebuking the river and throwing stones at it, pleading with it to turn back so that she can cross over to her son.

170   The title. The title and some of the imagery of this poem were suggested by Dürer's famous copperplate engraving, "The Knight, Death, and the Devil" (1513).

170   Line 2. Acritas is the warrior hero of the Byzantine epic, *Digenis Acritas*.

170   Line 17. Plapoutas and Nikitaras, heroes of the Greek War of Independence, were renowned for feats of great individual courage.

171   Line 5. Goetz von Berlichingen (1480–1562) was a German knight whose right arm was shot away in 1505 while he was assisting Albert IV, duke of Bavaria, at the siege of Landshut; he substituted an iron arm and became known as "Goetz with the iron hand." Goethe made him the hero of his play, "Götz von Berlichingen" (1771).

171   Line 20. The allusion is to Wagner's "Der Ring des Nibelungen."

A NOTE ABOUT THE EDITORS

Both EDMUND KEELEY and PHILIP SHERRARD have had a long-standing acquaintance with Greece. Mr. Keeley, who was born in Damascus, Syria, in 1928 of American parents, first went to Greece in 1936 when his father was assigned to Salonika as American Consul. Mr. Sherrard, born in Oxford, England, in 1922, was with the British Army in Greece towards the end of the war. Both are married to Greek girls, and have held academic positions in Greece for extended periods (Mr. Keeley twice as a Fulbright lecturer on leave from Princeton, where he now teaches; Mr. Sherrard as Assistant Director of the British School of Archaeology, a position he holds at present).

Greece has been of central importance in their separate literary enterprises: Mr. Keeley has written two novels with a Greek background (*The Libation,* 1960, and *The Gold-Hatted Lover,* 1961), and Mr. Sherrard has published three books about Greek culture and history (*The Marble Threshing Floor: Studies in Modern Greek Poetry; The Greek East and the Latin West: A Study in the Christian Tradition;* and *Athos, the Mountain of Silence*), as well as a volume of verse, *Orientation and Descent.* Their collaboration on this anthology began in 1956 on the island of Thassos and was completed after a sustained joint effort during the summer of 1959 at Limni, on the island of Euboea, where the Sherrards have a summer home.

April 1961

A NOTE ON THE TYPE

THE TEXT of this book was set on the Linotype in a new face called PRIMER, designed by *Rudolph Ruzicka*, earlier responsible for the design of Fairfield and Fairfield Medium, Linotype faces whose virtues have for some time now been accorded wide recognition. The complete range of sizes of Primer was first made available in 1954, although the pilot size of 12 point was ready as early as 1951. The design of the face makes general reference to Linotype Century (long a serviceable type, totally lacking in manner or frills of any kind) but brilliantly corrects the characterless quality of that face.

Composed, printed, and bound by
Kingsport Press, Inc., Kingsport, Tenn.
Paper manufactured by
Curtis Paper Company, Newark, Delaware.
Typography and binding design by
RUDOLPH RUZICKA